T0193941

I Kept My
Promise!

OZZY VERA

authorHOUSE®

AuthorHouse™
1663 Liberty Drive
Bloomington, IN 47403
www.authorhouse.com
Phone: 1 (800) 839-8640

© 2017 Ozzy Vera. All rights reserved.

No part of this book may be reproduced, stored in a retrieval system, or transmitted by any means without the written permission of the author.

Published by AuthorHouse 06/20/2018

ISBN: 978-1-5462-1424-3 (sc)
ISBN: 978-1-5462-1422-9 (hc)
ISBN: 978-1-5462-1423-6 (e)

Library of Congress Control Number: 2017916311

Print information available on the last page.

Any people depicted in stock imagery provided by Thinkstock are models, and such images are being used for illustrative purposes only. Certain stock imagery © Thinkstock.

This book is printed on acid-free paper.

Because of the dynamic nature of the Internet, any web addresses or links contained in this book may have changed since publication and may no longer be valid. The views expressed in this work are solely those of the author and do not necessarily reflect the views of the publisher, and the publisher hereby disclaims any responsibility for them.

Scripture taken from the New King James Version®. Copyright © 1982 by Thomas Nelson. Used by permission. All rights reserved.

Contents

AN OLIVE HAS TO GO THROUGH 3 STAGES FOR ITS OIL TO RUN.

IT HAS TO GO THROUGH THE SHAKING, THE BEATING AND THE PRESSING AND JUST LIKE THE OLIVE SOME OF YOU FEEL LIKE YOU WENT THROUGH THE SHAKING, THE BEATING AND THE PRESSING.

YOU WENT THROUGH ALL OF THAT FOR YOUR OIL TO FLOW.

NOW YOUR GREATER IS COMING!

COURTESY OF JEKALYN CARR'S ALBUM: GREATER IS COMING

THE COVER

Why did I choose this cover, there a 3 reasons why.

1. THAT DARKNESS
2. THOSE BIG HANDS
3. THAT ORCHID

I love my cover it's who I am all in 1, anyone who was privileged to have seen my cover before this book came out loved it. When I asked the photographer this is what I wanted for my book cover, he said he never did one of these, so I said there's always room to make more money. He did a fantastic job captured exactly what I wanted as well as my full shots in this book.

When I had my first fundraiser he volunteered his time at no cost and he never questioned it. So this is one of my THANK YOUS to him, please visit his studio if ever in Montclair, NJ and his website he's fantastic.

Portraitsbymichaelstahl.com

Interestingly enough 1 person said it should have a white background, I gave it some thought and decided it shall remain dark for it will take away from the statement I'm trying to make!

Whenever a client is referred or finds me to inquire about or purchase hair especially going through chemo. I end up seeing a darkness that envelops them I first saw this with my own aunt.

What I'm truly looking at is 2 questions: WHERE IS MY ANSWER and WHY ME?

MY HANDS: yes those are my big fat hands even in my own walk there was always helping hands that were guiding me through from all corners, I even thanked a majority of them publicly in this book.

THE ORCHID: Orchids are vulnerable, temperamental and require a' lot of PATIENCE to even get 1 bloom the roots are all in disarray they are air plants that's why the roots are outside of dirt, such a delicate flower.

This orchid was actually handed to me by a very sweet client that felt she couldn't make her re bloom; I told her I can do it!

When it was time for the book cover she had bloomed for the 5th time at this present time as I'm writing this chapter she's on her 6th bloom!

In retrospect this was actually my aunt's favorite flower, this is why I chose her.

MORAL OF THE STORY:

Through the darkness there will always be helping hands to handle such a delicate flower like you so you can re 'generate, re 'bloom, heal and be able to be beautiful again!

I KEPT MY PROMISE

"Hair loss affects people in different ways – some ignore it whereas others are devastated by it. For women suffering cancer, hair loss from the therapy can be the last straw. It can therefore make a huge difference to your life if you can seek help from someone who is compassionate, empathetic, and an expert in their field. Ozzy is such a person; he not only reassures the sufferer that their hair will eventually recover but helps them to look great while their hair is at its worst. And there is no doubt that looking good lifts the spirit enormously. Unfortunately, there are not many Ozzys around, which is why we are lucky that, with this book, we can learn from Ozzy's vast experience."

David Salinger
Director, International Association of Trichologists.

OZZY'S FOREWORD

This book is my personal journey as well as a guide for family, friends and stylist. When consulting, catering and just trying to understand a woman with hair loss while living with cancer.

All accounts in this book are very true; I've experienced each and every one of them. As well as how I view them from my perspective all the advice that is given throughout this book has worked for me,we are all created differently my walk may not be so comfortable in yours. However I do advise you to listen to the stories and gain insight into a rather tricky world a few of the stories may come off as harsh, that's how they were given to me.

I've added valuable information in this book, I had no clue I would keep on writing, I've never taken on a task like this somehow it was imbedded in me. I would be sleeping and writing in my sleep wake up with the chapter I was writing in my head, stay up extremely late into the night, just speaking to clients with conversations, that had nothing to do with the book, coffee shops, diners, restaurants just sitting on a bench trying to relax even in the movies on how I was going to write it the more I thought about each section the more the information and where to look came to me. Even commuting, riding to work the chapters kept coming.

You will discover much research and reliable sources throughout this book. I actually made it simple for the average reader to understand it. Even with all the information out there I find that it's never simplified for someone to understand. It's always handed out more impressively to be acknowledged rather than presented as a gift and here is the difference. When I first started volunteering for the American Cancer Society and would go to the treatments center I would notice magazines piled high for the patients to read interestingly enough the magazines remained piled high, never touched didn't matter which clinic I would walk into, they were actually reference magazines on cancer care. I would keep paying attention to the magazines each and every time. To let you in on a little secret when a woman is going through the last thing she wants to do is read up on anything that has to do with cancer. She wants this over and done with! Her life has just been interrupted.

So what did I do, I made it my business to read the magazine for these patients and my clients. I found what I was looking for a bevy of information on how to gain FINANCIAL HELP. I did read the magazines and they were more about finding treatment center where to go etc.

I also carry these magazines in my studio, however when I present these to my clients I specifically let them know why I chosen these for them I have the financial pages folded, so they go directly to the financial help. The response is they are grateful for the information and that I took time out to do the homework for them, why it was as if I handed them a gift. It wouldn't matter if my client has the resources or not they loved the idea I took time out to do this for them.

This can be a confusing, daunting and nerve wrecking time as I've written in this book many are financially strapped, do not know what advice to seek or where to look!

This book is written so you can be well equipped, know what to look for, what to expect and what questions to ask for as well so you will have the right to be treated fairly and with respect!

This book did not come easy, these are the answers I wasn't able to provide for my late aunt in her youth, all of this is her memory planted in me and how helpless I was to even guide her with the correct answer with just her hair.

NOW BECAUSE OF HER, YOU WILL BE WELL EQUIPPED!

At no time is anyone's name mentioned in this book within the stories to protect their identity, outside of friends, acquaintances that had served a positive purpose during this walk that at times may have been difficult.

The lessons taught throughout this book are all in the past have been forgiven, its water under the bridge, so that is where they are left. They were meant to be there for me, how else would this book have come to life? I look at them now and laugh they came off so silly to me.

If at any time anyone feels the negative stories are about themselves, then you must have some serious self-flattering going on and you will never know! HOWEVER' BECAUSE OF YOU it is able to EXIST!

May the stories within this book hold the key to your friends, aunts or mother's healing.

THROUGH HIS STRIPES WE ARE HEALED FOR THIS TOO SHALL PASS!

THE MURDER

It all started while meeting my new 8th grade class mate at WILSON AVE. SCHOOL that had just moved to Newark, NJ from New Rochelle, NY. I just so happened to be going into the principal's office that day when he was being registered, we had stood next to each other and instantly connected NO WORDS were needed. Not realizing that we would be inseparable from then on.

We would constantly be together each and every day. During freshman year of 1984 at East Side high school in Newark, NJ at 1st Period in Phys. ED one day he had asked me, let's skip school and go into the city (NY) so we could hang out. At that time the path (NJTRANSIT) was only 50 cents to ride into the city (NY) and I usually had 5 dollars on me so I had my round trip fare, as well as my lunch money which consisted of a slice of pizza and a soda typical for a teenager. This was months before I started a part time job.

We made sure we could get back home before school let out, we didn't skip school every day however it was enough that I had to make up classes for the remaining last 2 years of high school.

By JR. year Fernando had quit started going to beauty school and working retail it was obvious he hated high school. On the flip side he was a very creative person, he loved and adored BOY GEORGE of CULTURE CLUB so much during that time, that he actually resembled him which afforded him to acquire many retail jobs because of his look, his outgoing personality as well as get into many clubs in NYC because of this (my mother would've killed me if she would had found out). When we would just be at his house hanging out we always would be blasting the music from his bedroom window, what a fun memory, from time to time I still go into our old neighborhood to stay gazing at his window where he lived just to remember how fun that was.

By 16 I had landed my first job at ZARO'S bakery in Penn Station. Around that time I had to decide what is it that I wanted to do, I had just graduated from high school at 17, and since I had an inner desire to be fabulous it was either become a chef or get into hair (btw I'm an excellent cook).

Fernando was already in beauty school working retail and at a salon during the week, he really liked it. We were still hanging out in NYC at our usual spot THE PIERS, actually this area had become a sanctuary for us. I was already working making a living so around this time he had started persuading me to go to beauty school; He instinctively knew that I would be good at it.

It was at the NYC PIERS off of Christopher Street that we would talk about our future and how fabulous we would become.

During 1988 I was so consumed with working at a private corporate law firm, beauty school, as well as working retail in NY at a store called RECKLESS, the 2 owners had taken me in to keep me from hanging out at the piers and actually had become my mentors guiding me in the retail business world as well as working at a salon on Saturdays.

I was so involved work wise that Fernando and I weren't seeing each other as often. It was MARCH 19, 1988 a Saturday around 8 in the morning, I will never forget this day, the phone had rung and Fernando's mom had asked me had I seen or spoken to Fernando. I had told her that we only had spoken 2 weeks prior, but he should be home soon, this was odd he always got in from clubbing at 6 a.m. Like clockwork. It was interesting that when she had spoken to me and mentioned his name I had an overwhelming feeling that he was no longer with us. I had felt it in my spirit.

Come to find out Fernando was murdered 1 gunshot wound to his face and 2 in the back of his head. My life would not be the same. His murder was never solved and the case went cold 3/18/1988 it was a Friday he had passed exactly at 10:30 PM. They had found his body faced down under the breezeway of the baseball stadium in Weequahic Park, NJ that is no longer there.

So with this ammunition I decided to dedicate myself into the hair field so my part of the bargain would be fulfilled. To this day I do not stop thinking of him. This chapter is dedicated to his memory so he can always live. He was only 19.

I believe FERNANDO E. BARBOSA would have gone far in life, if this would not have happened especially in the entertainment world.

In Nov of 2015 I had visited his burial site, I was about 3 chapters into the book around this time, I hadn't been there since the 90's when I accompanied his mom.

WHAT A HORRIBLE YEAR THAT WAS when this tragedy happened!

Exactly 1 year later I was gifted by JEHOVAH JIRAH with a new friend that I had just happened to have met on a 1 800 # chat room that was popular during that time way before the internet. Instinctively we had clicked interestingly enough we had mutual friends and neither knew of the other go figure. We have nearly 30 years of friend ship if anything through this time we maybe had one disagreement and it wasn't all that from what I recall. We are totally different socially, individually and our social circles don't really match, however we totally understand each other. His name is MANNY MONROIG who has witness me do what I have told him what I was going to achieve. I truly believe he should focus on his singing especially since he has a great voice for being a balladeer. That's what he's naturally gifted with. So I thank him for always being supportive and never judging me!

He came at a time that was just right; I'm a loner to begin with though I know many people that year I really wanted to be left alone this murder made me look at people differently and distrust many.

You are truly my left lung even though you drive me crazy with that cell phone and those endless selfies OK! …..PATAH!

THE QUESTION

It was around 1990-1992 if only I knew then what I know now! How my life will change yet again.

I was 20 yrs. old around 1990 when things started being different with her. I didn't understand it at the time; I was just working at a salon. She would always visit on a Saturday afternoon from BROOKLYN; I always loved being under her wing when I would see her.

I love all my aunts all the same way but differently! So Liz and the Lucy better not get upset.

I don't quite remember much about the C talk so for the next 2 years this had become trivial. It did finally come up later on.

Not sure what to say nor do, I never asked questions and remained the same as always. HUGGING, KISSING AND TELLING HER, EVERYTHING IS GOING TO BE ALL RIGHT.

One Saturday, that I truly Thank GOD for and will never forget. I had come home right after work from the salon. To my surprise she was visiting my mother.

I came in, she was sitting at the kitchen table chatting away with my mom, around this time all was fine nothing seemed different as usual smiling.

She had teased me because I had wanted to go somewhere and didn't have a car so she said why you don't get a mule to haul your behind around like the rest of us had to do when we had no cars.

TRANSLATION IN SPANISH: BETE BUSCATED UNA JEGUAH PARA TE CARGE, since this is exactly how she said it.

I was so mad, I remember I had a loaded camera and as usual ready without hesitation I had asked my mom to take a picture of her and I. Now take into consideration I am 20 yrs. old 6'1 and told her I was going to sit on your lap and take this picture!

She had started laughing, from what I remember my mom had asked me why I wanted to take this picture it was no special occasion. My aunt just looked at me still laughing and had told me my behind was just way too big to be sitting on her lap. I in turn told her I want to take this picture so it can always remain with me. This is the only time I had taken a picture with her and I'm on her lap.

One day around 1 ½ yr. later she was visiting again, I came in my usual self.

HUGS, KISSES AND EVERYTHING IS GOING TO BE ALLRIGHT

But this time it was different and I knew it. I had just gotten home from working at the salon; she looked me dead in the eyes and asked me the most profound question that I will continue hearing for the rest of my breathable life.

This question has never changed and it stays the same, it continues to have the same effect all the time.

CAN YOU HELP ME WITH MY HAIR?

My answer: GO GET A WIG, wrong answer not knowing at that time what my answer had meant.

I did not realize how insensitive and what kind of impact this answer has on a woman who's about to undergo chemotherapy and begin to lose her hair!

I was young frivolous and what mattered was how fabulous I was going to become.

It was of all months around MARCH 15, 1992 also coinciding with the anniversary of FERNANDO'S death I will never forget it. The call came in my beautiful aunt had lost her battle and transitioned.

She has not died, she's resting and I will see her again!

I remember going to the funeral and just gazing at my grandmother standing over her casket not moving, I don't recall anything else.

I was young, in a new relationship at that time, not realizing what the future had in store for me.

The question never changes and always stays the same:
CAN YOU HELP ME WITH MY HAIR?
This entire book is dedicated to her loving memory and like my promise to Fernando I'm keeping my promise to her!
I am forever grateful for taking that picture that hangs in my private room in the salon; she has a huge smile on her face as she watches me assisting my clients with their new hair.
SO YES I CAN HELP YOU WITH YOUR HAIR!

The picture that follows is from my 1ˢᵗ fundraiser it included the picture of me sitting on her lap.
My first article in a magazine with the very 1ˢᵗ wig that I designed like 4 years prior that I used as a prototype for when clients came in to see, this was the unit I was never able to design for her.
And finally I gave the unit a cut and style like she would wear it and displayed it for the fundraiser.
This was all displayed in the front for all to see and so she can see me answering her question.

OPENING MY SALON

It was 2002; a new beginning for me I decided to spread my wings and open up my own salon. I was only 32 how funny of all months I had signed the lease in MARCH 2002!

It was just me my own finances and gut instinct. It was time to move on spread my wings and begin to fly.

When I had my grand opening ceremony everyone came out to celebrate I was grateful for all the gifts and enjoyed myself however this day left me a bit confused it was as if it was my wedding and funeral all at once after everyone left I sat there looking at all the plants and flowers I had received they started at the door and went all the way to the back of the shop for a week people were coming by to see what happened, however it left me somewhat melancholy and empty, years later when I had my first fundraiser I decided never to accept gifts like that anymore I would prefer those gifts to be monetary donations to go to someone who needs financial help with their healthcare bills. That will make me happy.

I have always been a loner and to this day prefer it that way. The impact of Fernando's death left me like this.

So I was by myself in my 1st salon, no one ever wanted to work with me and if they did it was because of an underlying agenda. So thank you JESUS for the gift of DISCERNMENT. I was and still am always ahead of these want to bees.

I loved being there all by myself always aware of the second set of footprints so really never alone, I prefer it that way.

My life has progressed and developed so much. I now understand why. I recall a person I had a long term relationship with saying to me prior to me opening this business.

INDEPENDENCE COMES WITH A PRICE OF LONELINESS

I never felt alone just different. Seven months into opening my business something interesting happened to me it never quite bothered me, however it became my thorn on my side and I just dealt with it the best way I could, focused on the book of JOB and started speaking over the problem.

I was a little confused but I just dealt with it. Grabbed the bull by the horns and kept it moving. Keeping in my thoughts GOD didn't bring me this far just to abandon me! As well as fed myself EXODUS 14:15 so I kept it moving.

My journey into additional hair was right around the corner; I ended up meeting with a very sweet and caring client around 2003 referred by another client that had moved away.

At that time I usually never paid much attention to women with thin hair. I just helped them out as much as I could. One day she just came in and had asked me OZZY do you think you can help me pick out a wig?

So without a thought I said sure. This is new to me and it seems like fun, and that's how I treated it, well around a week later I received a note to visit a woman in NYC to see if I was interested in getting involved with helping women with hair loss.

I found this intriguing shooked my head because there are no coincidences.

I called the number and made an appointment with her, I showed up, I was intrigued by the whole thing and stuck around. She had done something that kind of shocked me and at the same time made me laugh, I wasn't laughing at her it was her actions that were funny to me. She immediately took the caps from her mouth out, removed her hair stood in front of me and yelled:

DO YOU THINK I CAN WALK AROUND LOOKING LIKE THIS?

(BAYYYYYYYYYBEE) when I said I rolled, I rolled ok!

Right after that she had asked me the ultimate question that is continuously on repeat.

CAN YOU HELP ME WITH MY HAIR?

It was as if I was having an outer body experience. I completely froze, went blank and had traveled back in time to the year 1991-1992 remembering when my aunt had asked this of me. I was no longer looking at her; I was having a visit with my aunt.

That is when I knew and said to myself, I think this is what I'm supposed to be doing. So I took up the offer she had given me and I started becoming obsessed with the whole idea. As time went on one door lead to another, I began engrossing myself with any course that included additional hair.

Everything from knowing how to braid, creating a full wig from scratch, I found myself in a basement taking a course on wrap net weaving with an Asian instructor, flying all over the country for anything that dealt with hair replacement courses, even as far as studying with a HASIDIC WIG MAKER.

Little by little I started conquering all types of hair additions.

Before engrossing myself in any of this the person who had introduced me in the additional hair world had contacted me one day and asked if I can help her with a client. I told her I'll be away taking a class around that time, she demanded to know where I was going, I kindly said: you do not have a need to know card and I'm following your advice, if I wanted your advice I would need to pay for it, so I did and have all the certifications to prove it along with I do not like to be spoon fed, I like to eat with both hands!

There was only one thing that was missing, making sense and understanding all of this. Nothing truly connected with any of it. So I found myself asking questions, even though all along the answer was within me.

When this truly connected was when I started to think about my aunt. You see on the outside world everything was smiles and I'm ok. But what was she truly feeling when she was by herself, the thoughts that were going through her mind, the questions, the mortality and most importantly her feelings.

Once I started questioning all those feelings a flood of emotions enveloped me and began realizing how a woman thinks, especially how to connect emotionally which men are not used to doing.

I began to choose my word carefully as well as my speaking pattern. For each woman I encounter with hair loss, I'm revisiting my aunt.

A BIG BEAR HUG, KISS AND EVERYTHING IS GOING TO BE ALL RIGHT.

It never leaves me. I also add on THIS TOO SHALL PASS.

I have been in business on my own well over 15yrs and years on my own but not alone THE FOOTPRINTS ARE ALWAYS WALKING WITH ME!

As my momentum started picking up, I met one client on top of another. But none of this started happening until I understood the emotional aspect of it all and how deep it is.

I deal with all types of hair loss, from someone living with alopecia universalis, burn victim, trichotillomania (hair-pullers) and the list can go on.

The one that touches me the most is the client experiencing life with cancer because once we gaze into each other's eyes, I am having a visit, and it cannot be explained. It's bigger than me.

MY ACTIONS, TONE AND MANNERISM COMPLETELY CHANGE; I'm instantly in tune with her.

This experience is more than making a sale. The client is well aware she's coming to purchase something. However I choose to make it an experience to go as far as including her.

It's more than selling hair and making a profit. The visit is an experience, regardless of what's she's able to afford it's all treated exactly the same.

WHAT IS THE EXPERIENCE

For starters I'm not a regular wig salon. I am a CUSTOM DESIGN SPECIALIST which includes taking measurements, creating a template with the clients head, selection of hair it might involve blending, color, density and textures.

I do not like buying or purchasing stock pieces, this takes away from being creative and designing around the client's likes, wants and lifestyle. I love mixing the colors in the hair, that way when she is stopped everyone is trying to figure out, how did she get that color? I want to be able to draw attention to the hair and how beautiful it is. This is the GOAL, not attention to THAT WIG IS NICE.

I make sure I do not make this confusing to the client. I offer more options and explain everything to her in layman's terms, she becomes part of this. Unless she is a person who has worn hair before this will be all new to her it can become CONFUSING and DAUNTING!

My other goal is to remove all the ANXIETY that comes along with making a selection for new hair before she visits me.

When I receive a call from a new client, I make sure to do a quick consultation over the phone so when she gets to the salon, she is coming to get her HAIR DONE and not BUY A WIG (see the difference)

I do not want her coming to me without getting to know me first. I make sure I let her know I'm a STRAPPING TALL LATIN GUY standing at 6'1 easy on the eyes with EXOTIC HAZEL EYES (chuckle)

I want her to be as comfortable as possible upon meeting me reason being:

WHAT IS THIS MAN GOING TO DO WITH ME?
AND
HOW IS HE GOING TO ANSWER MY QUESTIONS?

Believe me these are the questions that are going through her mind.

This is why it's important for anyone involved in this to have a great website with plenty of original pictures a short but direct bio that gets to the point.

THE FUNDRAISER

Time passes on. It was time to start challenging myself after coming back from one of my hair loss conferences I decided to put together a fundraiser.

I started writing out my plan on my flight back considering I had 3 ½ hrs. To kill, enough time to write down all of my ideas.

How was I going to do this I immediately thought about what was included at the hair loss conference, however I had to format it in such a way that I would instead create a LIFESTYLE AROUND IT. I wanted it to be fun and cheerful with as much information as possible. That way any of my ladies would be able to walk away with something.

Throughout the whole process I just kept thinking of my aunt and how she would have felt about this whole Idea.

So I decided to put together a team and since I knew exactly what women go through during this time I had pieced it all together.

My team consisted of:

WENDY BROWNE: who explained lymphatic drainage and the importance of removing toxins from the body.

WWW.HIBISCUS.COM
37 WATCHUNG PLAZA
MONTCLAIR,NJ 07042
973-783-3381

MARVA SELEKA: the importance of skin hydration
WWW.BALANATURAL.COM
6 Midland Ave.

Montclair, NJ 07042
973-744-0028

SHAN MASSUCO: the effects of products full of chemicals, personal effects and the dangers of toxicity in them

WWW.SHANBEAUTY.COM
WWW.SOHEALTHYANDNATURAL.COM
605 BLOOMFIELD AVE.
MONTCLAIR, NJ 07042
973-220-3072
YouTube: SPOTLIGHT ON SHAN MASSUCCO
        SEPTEMBER 17-SHAN: SO HEALTHY AND NATURAL
        OWN IT VENTURES/NOV.30 2012 ROADSHOW-SHAN
        MASSUCCO

BENNY SANCHEZ: billing and insurance, how to file your claim

ALL SERVICE MEDICAL BILLING
1 BERLANT AVENUE
LINDEN, NJ
908-862-7118
SAMNAT123@MSN.COM

BETH DANNON: How clothing helped her cope through her ordeal and made a difference! Please visit her business page she sells great nostalgic pieces and funky clothing one of a kind pieces at: STUFFED CLOSET VINTAGE can be found on FB you can also visit her ebay online store WWW.STORES.EBAY.COM/STUFFED-CLOSET

I had 2 photographers
MICHAEL STAHL: event photographer
MICHAEL STAHL PHOTOGRAPHY
11 MIDLAND AVE.
MONTCLAIR, NJ 07042
WWW.PORTRAITSBYMICHAELSTAHL.COM
NATALIE BUSTAMANTE: #2 FREELANCE PHOTOGRAPHER

PAUL OF WWW.SWEETHOMEMONTCLAIR.COM
   WWW.PRETZELMENU.TUMBLR.COM
Who donated these delicious chocolate covered pretzels with rainbow sprinkles.
They were so yummy......

SAM: THE PIE STORE in UPPER MONTCLAIR who donated delectable treats
THE PIE STORE
100 WATCHUNG AVE.
UPPER MONTCLAIR, NJ 07043
973-744-4424
WWW.THEPIESTORENJ.COM
EMAIL: thepiestore@gmail.com

ILSON GONZALVES: SAMBA BRAZILIAN FARE downtown Montclair who donated delectable treats as well.
SAMBA
7 PARK STREET
MONTCLAIR, NJ 07042
973-744-6764
WWW.MONTCLAIRSAMBA.COM
And the woman who I would not have done this without, the only:

BARBARA LEMLY: IDENTITY IN DESIGN and part genius in putting it together
WWW.IDENTITYINDESIGN.COM
THANK YOU SO MUCH....
Included were a host of friends who had volunteered without a thought
THANK YOU.

I truly did not know what to expect, I threw myself into a pack of wolves expecting a mediocre crowd. Yes I was nervous, but what kept my sanity was the thought of my aunt sitting there smiling at me and the importance of making my mother and Aunt Liz proud at the end of the day it was for their sister, to keep her memory alive

So I had my team and this is when

OZZY AND FRIENDS

Had become a reality, I was expecting 30 people to show up and when I looked around there was almost 100. The women loved it went ballistic and I was the talk of the town.

Through all the ads, donation and raffle sales oh btw THE RAFFLE this is a must the women were like a hive of bees with all the goodies at the table, A DEFINITE MUST ALWAYS. They went coo coo with that, I HAD NO IDEA.

I was able to raise nearly 3,000 dollars and it was incredible. I couldn't believe it, this was better than throwing a birthday party! I was so happy, I challenged myself and won!

I highly advise anyone to do this, was it easy NO however it wasn't IMPOSSIBLE.

I'm sure someone had something ridiculous to say so if they did I CHALLENGE THEM TO DO THE SAME THING; you have 3 months to pull it together and raise 3,000 dollars.

I CHALLENGE YOU!

I've done it already and will do it again so I can double it.

This is not impossible even if you get a group of 30 people and have raised $300.00 dollars you've done something. SO DO IT

This is the time I figured out I had the power to take action and be of use somewhere else. I am able to get my hands dirty and MAKE IT HAPPEN!

This was one of my dreams and it became a reality, I can do it over and over again make it bigger than it can be, until I finally create a FUNDRAISING BALL

IT WILL HAPPEN

Time marches on: at the time I am writing this book it's 9-25-15, 10:20pm at my local STARBUCKS in Bloomfield NJ thinking about my future.

I'm thinking about what has transpired from 9-2014 till the present.

What a most difficult and trying 8 months at this time, I'm thinking about signing a lease for my new location which will be my 3rd salon, how funny that #3 again it's very significant to me!

Well let's backtrack, THANKSGIVING WEEK 2014 was not very

good to me, I was very upset with the breakup of my ex 3 weeks prior (OH WELL).

My Aunt GLORIA that was living in Puerto Rico had passed away Thanksgiving Eve. She always made great turkeys with ground beef stuffing so yummy. For her service I decided to create a custom silk floral arrangement with crystals she loved these kind of things: I LOVE AND MISS YOU TIA GLORIA

That thanksgiving eve, I was on the phone with a friend of mine JILL (aka) ANNIE OAKLEY we were chatting away carrying on laughing as well as making plans for dinner after the holidays with her husband, the following Monday her daughter called me first thing in the morning to let me know Jill had committed suicide. She was such a BEAUTIFUL PERSON.

Time moved on so around February 2015 the person that I was separated from had asked me if I can help them out with something, I said sure. This is where THE ACCUSATION ENTERS but that's for the next chapter.

It's APRIL 2015 at this time I was being filmed for a documentary by NADIRAH and QUENELL they had asked this of me 2 years prior, I had said yes. I totally forgot about it and the call came that it was time for my close up. I was filmed catering to a HAIR REPLACEMENT CLIENT. Throughout the whole process, I was thinking how is my life going to change this will be bigger than me.

I told Nadirah get ready you have opened up a CAN OF WORMS!

The night before the filming I had asked my client the main reason she had chosen and agreed to do this. Women are not just going to say yes to be filmed getting their hair done let alone a HAIR REPLACEMENT CLIENT.

Her answer: she wanted to tell her story about how frustrating and disappointing it was to go into salons to just get her hair done. When she started losing hers and it was getting thinner. The salons she was going to would start turning her away saying they couldn't do anything for nor help her, and if they did offer something she was not happy with nor it complemented her she never felt COMPLETE.

This is why I stress LISTENING, so many stylist are too busy trying to be THE ONE.

The one thing she wasn't happy with:

THE HAIR WAS WEARING HER, SHE WASN'T WEARING THE HAIR

SEE THE DIFFERENCE?

When I first met this client I had 3 strikes against me for starters:

- If everyone else turned her away how was I different?
- We are not of the same race, how would I begin to understand her.
- He's a MAN

I had asked her to take a seat; I casually started talking to her and had asked to tell me a little about you and to explain what her frustration was.

She finally opened up and told me, I had asked that I would need to see the REAL YOU! Can you please remove your HAIR not THAT WIG!

There she was expecting the dreaded answer, THERE'S NOTHING I CAN DO, however I answered as usual OH GIRL this is nothing we can make it happen, these are the necessary steps that we need to take and they'll be a number of weeks to wait for it, all I would need is 50% deposit to begin production

I answered correctly and said YES I CAN HELP YOU WITH YOUR HAIR.

I made her feel at ease, she took the steps waited patiently,finally her NEW HAIR came that I designed and created around her problem, placed it on,attached it to her existing hair turned her around and she said the magic words.

I'M LOOKING AT MYSELF!

Her true life testimony is on NADIRAH BELL AND QUENELL JONES documentary:

MY HAIR MY VOICE

THANK YOU for this blessed opportunity nothing is by luck or coincidence, it is through DIVINE INTERVENTION and it was meant to happen.

Again THANK YOU NADIRAH & QUENELL

LOVE YOU BOTH

MAY of 2015 had come around an I was going through my ups and downs tragedy struck again within a week and days apart, I had lost 2 old friends and I felt miserable.

One friend I hadn't seen in years before his death had started reaching out to me on FB. Manny and I couldn't believe it we were friends since the 80's. He was only 46.

Then the call came that my sweet angel LINDA had passed away as well just 54 yrs. old. I was devastated I had just seen her a week before an we were planning to go on a SEA TEA that is usually held throughout the summers on the Hudson, she just loved going with me from time to time.

I was horribly miserable and kept questioning myself,

WHAT IS THE POINT OF ALL OF THIS

It was just one disappointment in back of the other.

I had decided to reach out to the person that I had been separated from at that time and try to work things out with them so we can be back together, the answer was NO! OH WELL BYE FELICIA.

From May to June 2015, I wasn't feeling like myself, I began to hate everything even my own business, something that I truly loved.

It was as if I was being shaken back and forth but something interesting started to occur during all of this. I had begun to think about my father whom I had not spoken to in 8 years, I had totally dismissed him to the point that he was dead and buried. He was a total disappointment for most of my existing life so what was really the point to even acknowledge him.

So from the months prior to my 2 friends passing a way before the hair loss conference that was quickly approaching in July, I had kept thinking about him all the while all was chaotic around me.

I'm very good at holding face to the point you wouldn't even know, I started questioning myself and remember what Jesus stated in scripture and had done on the cross:

If I don't forgive him, he won't forgive me and I will be standing in shame in his presence!

This was the one thing that held the key to the door that was about to be opened in the coming year as well as move forward. Here I am again at Starbucks writing all this down on this legal pad.

Before any of this everything was going to end!

The hair loss conference was fast approaching.

Out of the blue I had decided to call my father and clear the air with him. In truth the plan was to surprise him in Puerto Rico around Nov. and not call, however my spirit spoke to me and said that's not a good idea he needs to hear your voice first.

So I called and my stepmother had answered, she couldn't believe it we talked for a while and caught up, she had asked me if I wanted to speak with my father, I said that's why I'm calling.

He nearly fainted and couldn't believe it he said he has been waiting for my call was crying and had begun to apologize for everything, I had to silence him. I had called to make my peace and release my anger of him and towards him. This was the key that was affecting the door that is about to open. He heard it from my own voice and into his ears that way that was done and out of the way.

You see if I wouldn't have acted on it or had spoken to him, yes I was going to Puerto Rico, November 2015 not to see him alive but at his funeral . I would've lived in regret. This was the reason he started coming to me months prior and the vision that was given to me.

You see forgiveness is not for that person it's for you! After all that it was as if the load I was carrying fell off my shoulders. Boy I was not expecting what was coming next.

I was going to the HAIR LOSS CONFERENCE soon but before that I had to go through another hurdle.

ENTER THE ACCUSATION!

I would like to thank ANDREA HAYDEN owner of
THE HAIR MANAGEMENT GROUP
13214 HUEBNER RD,
SAN ANTONIO, TEXAS`
1-210-558-3222
www.andreahayden.com

We'll talk about her later, as well as BARBARA PICKENS owner of
THE SANCTUARY
THE PLACE OF RESTORATION
217 WEST STONE AVE, #A
GREENVILLE, SC 29609
1-864-881-1451

1-864-241-21

<u>www.thesanctuarysalon1.com</u>

Who like a mother had said BOY GET YOURSELF TOGETHER, we're going to have a blast at conference, and you weren't lying.

Please visit their clinics if ever in need of TRICHOLOGY SERVICES and or ADDITIONAL HAIR both are experts in their fields.

FIVE MAIN CAUSES OF CANCER

- TOO MUCH SUGAR
- LACK OF VITAMIN D
- POOR NUTRITION LACKING IN AMINO ACIDS AND TRACE METALS
- LACK OF OXYGEN AND EXERCISE
- SEVERE SHOCK AND STRESS

ANDREA HAYDEN AND OZZY

BARBARA PICKENS AND OZZY

MY LIFETIME FRIEND MANNY …..…

BEING FILMED FOR MY HAIR MY VOICE

THE ACCUSATION

So I decided to accept the deaths of my two friends as well as the ones prior, 4 deaths of friends that were very close to me.

A big THANK YOU as well to JEREE WADE owner of
SERENITY SEMINARS, LLC
605 BLOOMFIELD AVE. SUITE 1
MONTCLAIR, NJ 07042
1-973-509-0374
WWW.SERENITYSEMINARS.COM
LOVE YOU DOLL

In late June I had decided to reach out to the person that I had been separated from, now going back to the February before anything occurred they had asked a favor of me.

A friend of theirs was undergoing chemotherapy treatment and living with cancer. They had wanted to know if I would design a custom unit for her. I said sure not a problem.

I had asked that if this was the case I would like to speak with her have her reach out to me so I can hold a quick consultation over the phone, she knew who I was and I knew who she was but we never had met physically.

I'm not sure about the circumstances here and what was said between them or if it was even true that this person just wanted to do this lie about it just to be facetious with me. And if this was the case THANK YOU for the IDEA.

I'm also not sure if they were purchasing the hair for her or helping her out financially with this.

So here's a bit of advice for anyone considering doing this for a client, friend or family member. Unless she asks this of you,

DO NOT TAKE CONTROL OF HER PROBLEM, CAPEEEESH

This will be explained further in the book.

ADVISE TO STYLIST WHO IS INTERESTED IN CONSULTING WITH THIS CLIENT!

The reason I had asked to speak with her before she came to my studio was so I can ease her ANXIETY, CALM HER NERVES AND REASSURE HER

- She doesn't know me
- She's angry you won't know but she is
- So she can feel as if she's getting her hair done
- all her inhibitions would have been left at the door

THIS NEVER HAPPENED!!!!!!!!!!!!!!

So in late June 2015, I decided to text his person again about his friend. So here's where the accusation enters THE FRAY.

ME: Hey hope all is well, btw out of curiosity did your friend ever decide to do anything with her hair, is she wearing hair, walking around w/a scarf, is she okay being comfortable with just a hat? The offer still stands on the table and I am more than happy to answer any questions and help her out.

THEY: For your information she has already gone through her 6 months of treatment and it's over with and BECAUSE OF YOU she was WALKING AROUND BALD #1

ME: I'm not sure what you mean by that, it seems a bit pointed and mean spirited, how am I the cause of her problem

THEY: Well she wouldn't feel comfortable around you and I told her what you did, not sure what it was, it just wouldn't be right that's why SHE'S WALKING AROUND BALD BECAUSE OF YOU #2

ME: I'm not sure where you are going with this but I really don't know this person, I know of her but don't know her secondly why is she involved in anything that went on between us this is really bad and I'm not owning it.

THEY: This is not a good idea, you don't know how to act around people, you are irreverent, I don't want to be around you nor am I interested in you, it's best that you leave me alone and this is why SHE'S STILL WALKING AROUND BALD, BECAUSE OF YOU #3

I really felt hurt behind this and it was a bit shocking, regardless I had to make a decision and I'm glad I chose the LATTER

ME: I'm sorry you feel this way you do not ever have to worry about me again, I can forgive you for this, on knowing I do not own this accusation. We not even need to see each other again, say hi etc.

But I promise you this 1 thing; I truly want you not to believe me and actually think of it as a joke. SO DON'T BELIEVE IT! I do not own being the cause of her problem, however I promise you,

YOU SHALL STAND IN MY PRESENCE IN FULL REGRET

And I left it at that and moved on. (EXODUS 14:15)

To the person who I was accused of you walking around BALD, it's a shame they used your condition to use it against me and if that's a friend to you what's the point of having an enemy ….MOVING ON.

This all sounds looks a bit ridiculous and childish when I reflect on it, however I opted to include it, hopefully it will encourage someone who's ever been dogged out you will see what a great Idea this will become as you read along. I have let go of this anger a long time ago this no longer bothers me and has been forgiven, it has been released but trust very much like TINA TURNER I decided TO KEEP MY NAME!

For these parts I'm dedicating to my cousin BETSY.

STORY TIME

Here's a little story of REGRET 5 have stood already in my presence, I can see what lies ahead #6…..

Many years ago I had a client; this person is no longer with me. They had called me on a Tuesday afternoon, I was working on some papers and ready to leave early, I usually tell this story because it's very interesting to me, I always reflect on it as a point of reference!

I answered the phone, THEY: oh hi, what're you doing, I don't know I must've been twiddling my thumbs not sure, I said just getting some things done and about to run out to get these errands out of the way.

THEY: well I need my hair done

ME: I said ok, but I'm running out so would you like to make an appointment.

THEY: why can't I come now?

ME: UHM, I'm on my way out

THEY: WHERE ARE YOU GOING?

ME: I do not think you have a need to know card!

I found her ridiculous at this point.

So I kindly responded if you've called for an appointment make it, I'm on my way out come in the morning.

THEY: she replied with one of my favorite sayings that just proves HOW IGNORANT anyone who comes off as upper crust ended up resembling a dog that vomits and then returns to the vomit to lick it up and eats it ! YOU KNOW YOU WANT MY MONEY! At this point they had become A TURD!

I in turn looked at the phone and introduced her to the NJ CLICK! (I HUNG UP ON HER) the sense of ENTITLEMENT got the best of her!

A year or so had passed I received a call from this person, can she come see me I need to tell you something, she came with her husband as a buffer …EVS! Only my AUSSIE friends down under understand this term………

She revealed to me she had BREAST CANCER, will be undergoing treatment and WILL BE LOSING HER HAIR… guess who the WIG MAKER WAS, so I just looked at her never mentioned a word. I said I will get back to you it was about 4 days before I spoke with her again. She called wondering why I didn't reach out to her (tones where different now). I just had to absorb this whole thing and think about it, I find it quite interesting for someone to be so ignorant say you want my money especially when common sense indicates I'm in business to make money, not acting like you're doing me a favor and get to this point.

So I had her come in took her measurements, guided her reassured her and designed the most fabulous unit I could conjure up at the end of the day I was being creative, loved it and that to this day I still receive calls for. I also was the person that ended up cutting all her hair down she was crying through this whole process, I usually hate this part I prefer not to do it unless they're ready for it, but when her new hair came in it was FABULOUS and no one was the wiser.

MORAL OF THE STORY: which I think about all the time when the folks want to act up.

DO NOT REPAY, VENGEANCE IS MINE SAITH THE LORD ...I SHALL REPAY.

You see I never mentioned anything about the incident, she knew she was in the wrong, but it was ok! For these kind of circumstances, I usually sit back lay low become practically nonexistent get a bag of popcorn and enjoy THE SHOW, in the end it's always a show.

THE GAPS

Enter the false promise, huge gaps can exist when false promises are being given out, take for example an older woman who is told she will be losing her hair where she is receiving her treatment THE HOSPITAL, refers her to the wig store that they highly recommended.

When listening to this story and interviewing this woman's daughter all the problems where coming together as she remembered her mother's ordeal!

The mom had been referred by the hospital to this wig salon to purchase her new hair, she was so excited that they had referred her that she felt there was no need to worry (THE ESTABLISHMENT) referred her.

Upon going to her appointment at the salon she met with the owner/stylist they sat her down found a short unit for her to try on she felt comfortable with, they took the measurements and needed to order this one for her. At no time was she given the proper consultation, the owner of the salon told her that if she wanted that unit she would need to pay for it up front the price was $500.00, the client was on a fixed income at no time was not asked if she had insurance coverage to reassure her that they will reimburse her.

They just told her if this is the one you want this is how much it cost you will need to pay for it so you can have it before your hair starts falling out!

Out of guilt and embarrassment the client paid for it right there and then she felt blindsided and seriously taken advantage of, they played on her age and sweet talked her into it.

It was a DOWNHILL SPIRAL on making any other purchases.

Upon waiting for her new hair to come she was told, that she would need to get a mastectomy on one of her breast and that she would need to buy a special bra the cost $150.00 again the HOSPITAL referred her, here was a new burden to deal with after feeling taken advantage of by the wig salon.

She refused to buy the bra and opted to wear her usual ones that she stuffed with socks.

Finally the new hair came in she went to pick it up accepted the fact she paid for what else could go wrong let's go. Her 2 daughters went with her.

Upon trying on the unit she paid for she immediately said it felt to tight, #1 daughter just wanted her to be happy the other noticed all the flaws especially how small the unit looked on her and was way too small for her head, it was way above her ears.

The salesperson told her it was measured to the exact size of her head and there was nothing that could be done.

The mother didn't say anything and left on the way back in the car she was wearing her hair not saying a word staying silent (indication she had a lot on her mind) was obviously unhappy! The one daughter kept noticing that the hair was rising and lifting all the way home from the salon.

The other daughter went home and the other stayed with her at the house time for the showdown at the ok corral, who is going to speak 1st!

The mother told her it was a waste of time and is not wearing THAT HAIR. It was way too tight, small and it hurt. She also felt obligated to wear the hair around the other daughter when she was around so she would pin the hair down on the wig liner so it wouldn't lift. Also felt as if she needed to be the spokesperson for Tylenol from the pain.

Time past and came to terms with the unit, still felt it was a waste of money, the hair ended up in a box in the closet.

She was so disheartened about the whole thing she decided to continue her chemo treatments at her primary doctors office who performed the mastectomy never to go back to that hospital, felt that they sold her a false promise, refused to wear that hair that she wasn't happy with and from then on decided to just get her treatments in full make up and dressed to the nines, this was what was compensating for not wearing the hair, it made her happy and made her feel especially strong. Dealing with that! B.D.H. private joke

SO HERE'S WHERE EVERYTHING WENT WRONG

The relationship between the hospital and the wig salon, a HUGE GAP was obviously there.

The additional hair store that has a referral relationship with the hospital should have:

1. An adequate informative pamphlet for the hospital on how the consultation is going to go before the client comes in to make a selection.
2. The wig salon owner should be knowledgeable and hold a short consultation over the phone to ask the client specific questions:
   A. Are you aware that insurance/Medicaid cover a certain percentage, please check with them first.
   B. There's going to be a 2 week wait for the unit.
   C. Before making this decision what kind of budget are you working with, maybe I can offer you an option from low to high
   D. And the units cost from such and such to this price

DO NOT IMMEDIATELY START PITCHING A SALE, SEE WHAT HAPPENED.

If the trial unit was what she felt comfortable with when she was trying it on, that was a sign that just order that size with the color and density she would like. SIMPLE.......don't get puffed up because the hospital referred you .... DIDN'T TAKE INTO CONSIDERATION THE GAP AND HOW SHE LEFT FEELING ....

When it came time for the operation she let her daughter know again she wasn't going to BUY THAT BRA, they just want my money and take advantage of me! *ANYWAY WHO WANTS THESE TITTIES* her words not mine

SO HERE'S TO ALL THE IRMA'S, there are reputable businesses out there you just have to seek them out. So I'll help you out with this one ok.

Enter JOHARI'S in MONTCLAIR, NJ

WHAT TO DO WITH
MY BREAST NOW

Let's be real, right now is an extremely stressful time for you, and it's only natural for you to feel this way. We have a love/hate relationship with our breasts, our hair, and how our body ages. When stricken with illness, it can put you on a roller coaster ride of emotions.

My name is Deborah Furr, the owner of Johari; a bra fitting boutique located in Montclair, NJ. I have worked in the industry for 36 years, 16 of which I have focused on properly fitting women into bras. I will say, I've seen it all. I get women who are happy when they learn their true size and I also I get anger and tears when I tell a woman something she doesn't want to hear (like a much larger cup size than she ever imaged).This has made me realize our breasts play a strong role in our lives. Breasts for many women area extension on how we feel about self image, for some it's a sense of empowerment, for others, they're a headache. They are a source of food for our newborn babies, they are a sexual toy for our partners, whichever way you view them, and they play an important part in our lives.

My role as a bra fitter is to make your breasts look the best they can. After a certain age our breasts will change shape and size. Your bra size will change many times over your lifetime. A proper bra fitting can take years off your appearance. I've learned over the years to accept how my body looks, and that it's all about accentuating the positive and camouflaging what I may think is negative.

Over my bra fitting years, working with women with breast cancer has been more common than I would like to admit. Whether you have had a full mastectomy, lumpectomy, or one breast removed with or without breast reconstruction; in order to feel whole again, the proper bra fitting will make you feel like your old self. After a diagnosis of cancer, I'm finding that most women go for reconstruction surgery and prosthesis may not be needed. Most women are naturally smaller on one side than the other, and the right fitting bra will camouflage that. In some cases, a small pad is added to create the appearance that each breast is the same size. Because bras are designed to hug your body, you will find that you no longer need a bra with a sewn in pocket.

I must say if you underwent reconstruction surgery, your breast tissue has been reshaped and the surgeons today are doing amazing work. When a woman comes into Johari for a bra fitting it is usually right after surgery. We fit her into a comfortable non-underwire bra that she will wear while the healing process takes place; time may vary from 6 months up to a year before going into an underwire bra. Yes, you can wear an underwire bra again. Most women are wearing the wrong size bra, meaning the wire digs and pokes in places where it shouldn't. If you are properly fitted, you should not feel the underwire and you can go back the wearing pretty bras again.

A bra fitting is an important step for you, and I must stress to seek out a bra fitter who is compassionate, kind, and will listen to your needs. She will find you a bra that fits your needs and body type. Keep in mind, even if you choose to have prosthesis in your bra with a proper fitting, there is no need to sew in a pocket, and you can go back to wearing the type of bras you liked and wore prior to surgery.

Deborah Furr
Johari
76 CHURCH STREET
Montclair, NJ 07042
973-744-8070.
Joharionline.com

ANDREA

What can I say about Andrea we met nearly if I'm accurate 13 years ago and of all place's a hair loss conference in Florida. It was actually Andrea and two other women that were sitting together. I never said much to them on that they stood out to me.

I remember in the first class that we were in, they were sitting toward the back on my left side and I was all the way in the front, I would keep turning around to look at them, since I knew right then and there we would automatically be friends.

I made it my business after that class to chat up a storm. That conference was over with, I returned to NJ an around 5 months later I decided to go back to Florida for a woman's hair replacement 3 day course. I signed in sat down lo and behold Andrea and the other 2 women were sitting directly in front of me, so we ended up looking at each other and smiled. At this conference we had just exchanged info and said we would keep in touch, it was another 3 or 4 months I booked another course for something else flew back to where I was going to be taking the classes and BOOM Andrea and the other 2 women were there we started laughing and accused each other of stalking.

I am not one for luck or coincidence so we had made a pact since the 4 of us seemed serious about investing in our education and learn as much as we could, so that whenever something new would pop up we would take the courses together.

I cannot even keep up with all the money we had spent on learning but here we are 13 years later.

The other 2 women I do not mention in this book, they had seemed to drop out and not be as interested as Andrea and I had become. However

Andrea and I continued to fulfill a vision, even though we're experts under the umbrella of hair we wanted to meet some goals and at this time we did.

She fulfilled her mission of directing the IAT Conference something she had spoken to me about years prior that was 1 of her goals and it came to be, and guess what one of my goals was to be, you guessed it, to be in front of a very large group speaking about what I'm passionate about!

This is why I connected with her so well; I knew it from the moment I set my gaze on her we would be connected spiritually.

One feature that attracts me the most that she has a habit of doing is when she is expressing herself she extends her hand and naturally sticks out her pinky, the same way my mother does this always had caught my attention.

She's not the easiest person to get a hold of; however she had come through for me when I was at a low point. I love her for that we will never be separated!

My vision has come forth through her being a part of my life, she was the connection that linked the chain to give birth to the one thing I have been craving for such a long time and BECAUSE OF YOU ANDREA HAYDEN ...

IT HAS COME TO LIFE......

GOING TO CONFERENCE

It's already mid July 2015, I'm heading to the IAT HAIR LOSS CONFERENCE that was being held in Washington, D.C. for the very first time.

I was so happy because that meant no connecting flight for me, I made my peace with my father had accepted the deaths, was processing this accusation and what was I going to do with that, it was given to me 3 times for a reason.

I decided, OWN IT and create something with this.........

I was excited to see my friends from throughout the country, DC and just enjoy my time. There were so many new faces as well; however once you get to know me it'll be very hard to forget me. It was a 2 day conference but I chose to stay for 5 days.

For one of the days I wanted to visit THE HILLWOOD ESTATE which is a must.

A year prior I had promised DAVID SALINGER the ceo/president of the IAT CONFERENCE, that I would love to take him and his wife SUE there as a gift for traveling all the way from Australia.

This is something I truly enjoy doing. Many of my friends aren't aware that I love visiting botanical gardens and mansions. That's such a huge part of who I am. It would be a dream to do a book signing during the month of the orchid show in honor of my late aunt that was her favorite flower.

The day was gorgeous and we went about our business, I was not prepared for what was going to transpire during lunch. You see David and Sue didn't have a clue of the turmoil and disappointments I had endured the months before. I for the most part am a very private person when it comes to my emotions, and can hide them very well.

The main reason I wanted to take them there to this elaborate mansion, because the prior year David was visiting Philly for a smaller conference not sure if it was an introduction to the Trichology association or the classes that were being offered through them.

I really had shown up to surprise both he and Andrea since I was only 1 hr. away. I must've have arrived at the right time since I wasn't aware of what had transpired prior to my visit. But I must have brought some relief.

David was really happy to see me but what was interesting he sat right next to me had briefed me on the buffoonery that had gone on before I arrived. I felt so embarrassed for him. I quickly changed the subject and asked if Sue and he would be interested in visiting the HILLWOOD ESTATE? I would love to take them there as a gift, for traveling so far.

At the present conference 2015 he remembered the promise and we went. Around lunch time at THE HILLWOOD ESTATE David had asked me how I felt about the conference. I in turn told him it was very strong this year and enjoyed it very much. But there's one thing missing and I have noticed this in many conferences outside of this one as well.

How to understand and cater to a woman who is losing her hair, while living with cancer.

Remember she's also a HAIR LOSS CLIENT! I had told him that it is imperative to understand she is dealing with four things that seriously need to be addressed:

- A DEGENERATIVE DISEASE
- PSYCHOSOMATIC ISSUES
- MALNUTRITION
- HAIR LOSS

And guess which one of these this person will be worried about the most, you got it. HAIR LOSS

What was also interesting to me at this meeting? The prior evening a client had sent me an incredible review about the 2 new hair systems she had purchased from me and how pleased she was. *(read insert at end of chapter)

I had asked David and Sue to read it, to add to this Suburban Essex Magazine a NNJ magazine had sent me a congratulatory award and recognition this was my 6th award. I couldn't believe it these things were synchronized in such a way that couldn't have been questioned.

For one I do not believe in luck or coincidences this was DIVINE INTERVENTION.

It was funny because David looked at me and said I do not need further proof.

I KNOW WHO YOU ARE! You will be one of our guest speakers for the conference July 2016.

DO YOU HAVE YOUR POWER POINT PRESENTATION TOGETHER?

I had not absorbed any of this and without hesitation I said YES, I will do it. At the same time he had asked me would I be interested in guest speaking at the conference in October 2016 in NEW ZEALAND can you do this?

I couldn't believe what I was hearing, and I couldn't quite absorb it I had just said yes to both. At the time I'm writing this its 9/26/15 10pm I'm in my room.

What was my future going to hold for me? I thought about how I wasn't going to the conference from being so upset and how THAT ACCUSATION was bothering me.

What was I going to do with this accusation? I was still dealing with this and had said yes to the lectures.

I mentioned nothing to no one and seriously couldn't believe it!

One thing I did know for sure releasing and forgiving the hatred and anger I had towards my father made this all possible. So I'm thankful for making that decision.

The promise to my AUNT and FERNANDO is about to be FULLFILLED in 2016.

YES I CAN HELP YOU WITH YOUR HAIR AND WE'RE GOING TO BE FABULOUS

It's really happening; the documentary I was filmed in will coincide and be hopefully released during this time. I started to think about all of this.

What is my future going to hold things are about to change and this bucket full of water is going to fall on me.

It's interesting that for someone who was accused of being

IRREVERANT and does not know how to act around people was offered this. But it was

BECAUSE OF YOU……..

David was put in my path through Andrea they were selected a long time ago!

So I got in touch with a good friend of mine DIANA. I was aware of her professional background inquired some advice, I said GIRL I need to get this power point presentation together, flew into a frenzy wrapped it up and this is how …..

FINDDIANA.COM

Was born, I went nuts and I found her. (Chuckle)

But this accusation still hung over my head even though I didn't own it. I needed to do something with it since it was given to me 3 times.

So I started thinking long and hard.

I KNOW EXACTLY WHAT I'M GOING TO DO WITH THIS ACCUSATION

You see I had a decision to make either I was going to have a PITY PARTY over this or I was going to use it as a tool and turn a negative into a positive.

I had started dissecting every hateful and negative thing that was thrown in my direction via text that person had said.

So I started with comparing the two of us mentally

- I had the nerve an drive to open up my own business at 32 and have been on my own for 15yrs. SELF EMPLOYED thank you
- The decisions I make are not based on emotion they're analytical
- I am in a position to be able to change someone's life for the better
- I am capable of pulling together a fundraiser with a team of people to raise money
- I am in a position of power and can influence people.
- I have been given and chosen for this platform.
- WHAT HAVE YOU DONE?

Since I have the power to raise money, I have chosen to create a

BECAUSE OF YOU LINE

That is in the works at the time I'm writing this, I have started with a line of T-shirts.

BECAUSE OF YOU I AM STILL HERE

15% of the proceeds within the property of BECAUSE OF YOU will go to the CANCER ASSOCIATION of my choosing, as well as through any OZZY AND FRIENDS EVENT.

There will be a number of other BECAUSE OF YOU items that will be created as I go along.

The t-shirts can be custom ordered on my site www.ozzyshairart.info through pay pal make sure when purchasing attach a note with your full info size and address. Thank you

10% of the proceeds from this book will also go to the CANCER ASSOCIATION of my choosing.

You see what this person had meant for EVIL GOD MEANT FOR GOOD.

So this is my future goal through any OZZYANDFRIENDSEVENTS as well as the BECAUSE OF YOU LINE

THE DREAM THAT WILL HAPPEN

Here I am again 9/27/15 11:22am, I am back at the Starbuck in Bloomfield, NJ drinking one of my favorites THE VERY BERRY TRENTI. I usually like to sit in the back facing out because I like to envision myself leading. It also places me in a position of power! Wouldn't it be great to hold my 1st signing here since this has been such a place of refuge to focus on writing this book. Each night I wrote 5 to 10 pages here and this too will happen.

Now on to the dream I am talking about, what dream is this? Now with all that is going to transpire within the next year and all the access I will have I would like to create a division within the CANCER SOCIETY to cater specifically to single mothers raising their children who are living with this temporary condition and yes it's temporary, who have no support system, are especially financially tied and feel as if there is no hope. Even if it's 1 woman at a time.

Though what I am able to do is for women all across the board. This woman is my main goal, that way there will be something for her, from paying for a car service to her doctor's apt., groceries etc. just to make things a little easier for her. Life is already a bit difficult at times.

STORY TIME

This one's dedicated to my pumpkin DEBBIE MALINOSKI and her cousin DIANE
Debbie owns a fabulous women's boutique
HIPNOTIQUE
111 W. MARION AVE.
PUNTA GORDA, FLORIDA

1-941-347-7250
www.hipnotique.net

Everyone plays an important part in this game we call life. So I will make this short and sweet.

Debbie had referred her cousin Diane to me to help with acquiring new hair since she was about to lose hers from the cytotoxic drugs. I had created a really bright red unit that to my surprise actually came out great and matched her personality perfectly, I was skeptical at first since I want everything to be perfect and not draw to much attention. I'm not sure if her family or Debbie were aware of this, but one day she had called me and asked if I could help her with something, I said sure go for it!

She began to tell me about a young lady maybe late 20's early 30's that she knew was struggling financially and had 2 small children was diagnosed and about to start treatment and above all else lose her hair.

Diane had asked me how much would it cost for a regular unit so she can have hair, I told her. I just needed to see a picture of her and I'll take it from there.

A couple of weeks followed I had the new hair coincidentally it just happened to be about 3 weeks before Christmas. I called her to come and pick it up, but 1 thing I did ask her, I would like to know specific details about the young lady and what was really going on. So she told me with all that Diane was going through already she did not make it about herself. Diane came to pick up the new hair she was about to pay for it and I told her you cannot pay for this.

This will be my gift to you and in turn it will be your gift to her, what she didn't know I had placed an envelope with some money in the box with a note, so when the young lady opened it, it would fall out. It wasn't much however it was enough to bring a smile to her face and brighten her darkness!

So the moral of the story:

Diane's transition was not in vain she had transitioned THANKSGIVING MORNING 2014 and BECAUSE OF YOU I was able to help this young lady out, this is one of the main things that fueled my passion for this goal.

WHY IS IT IMPORTANT TO ME?

I want to do this no one or anything can persuade me to do anything else

I want to be a voice and be supportive for this specific woman

I will challenge every man who reads this book to donate to the cause!

Let me be the one to get my hands dirty, they are always full of chemicals and color anyway

It doesn't matter if you have a big corporation or work at a store and have had a desire to do something and didn't know how to go about it.

WELL HERE I AM YOUR POSTER BOY

And BECAUSE OF YOU I will be able to do this. All you have to do is donate to the cause and HELP.

ESPECIALLY all the men who grew up without a FATHER FIGURE in the home.

I'M SPECIFICALLY CHALLENGING YOU SO YOU TRULY UNDERSTAND what I'm talking about!

(MY CLIENTS REVIEW)

A few years ago I lost my hair due to chemo therapy. A friend had referred me to OZZY, but I never brought myself to going. Instead, I purchased a few wigs from the local wig stores and I was satisfied with the way that I looked. I had hair on my head and no one would be the wiser. Eventually, my hair grew back and everything was good… for about the year, my cancer was back and I was facing chemo again. My friend reminded me again to go to OZZY, and this time I did.

It was perfect timing. I met with OZZY a few weeks back to have 2 wigs custom made. The wigs came just in time because my hair started to fall out. The wigs were beautiful! They are very light weight and extremely natural looking. The fact that he asked questions, listened to what I had to say, examined my hair combined with his expertise and knowledge, he delivered a wonderful product. A few days later I met a new oncology nurse and I was wearing my new wig. She asked me if I had started to lose my hair yet…. I laughed and told her that I was wearing a wig. This is a TRUE testament to OZZY'S WORK.

OZZY is a professional. He is passionate about his work. He is knowledgeable. OZZY explains everything to you in a manner in which you can understand. So don't be afraid to ask questions, he is patient and he wants you to understand.

OZZY is personable and very easy to talk to.

The moral of this story is: do not settle, don't HESITATE and don't be afraid to. CALL OZZY

MY DEDICATION
OF MY DREAM

The one woman I'm dedicating this passion and dream, she is:

THE ROSE IN THE GARDEN, THE CREPE MYRTLE THAT STANDS ALONE

THE IRIS THAT IS IN FULL BLOOM, THE DINNER PLATE DAHLIA

THE ILLAWARA FLAME TREE, THE ALPINIA, THE ANNUAL DELPHINIUM

THE BLEEDING HEARTWINE, THE CATASETUM, THE FRANGIPANI

THE LAELIA, THE MAXILIARIA

And the list can go on and on (she will have to look at all these plants up)

My parents were separated when I was 4 years old I grew up in a single parent home with NO FATHER FIGURE, even though she never kept him away from us, he was a total disappointment my entire life!

But that was ok, I made my peace and have let it go!

Life wasn't always perfect. But in my eyes through hers it was and I always knew a change was going to come.

I don't recall never being fed, clothes on my back, I didn't have a bike, roller skates, skateboard, able to go to a private school nor the easy bake oven I was desiring! She was actually very strict raising my brothers and me by herself.

You see she raised 3 gifted men even though there was struggles we were raised with the aggression, tenacity and drive to be able to stand out, be seen as 1 and be able to be self-reliant!

In truth in my eyes I didn't miss out on anything had everything and life was perfect because GOD CREATED HER PERFECT and she is my MOTHER!

And BECAUSE OF YOU I AM ABLE TO HELP THESE WOMEN OUT

I LOVE YOU ABOVE AND BEYOND

VIDA

translated means LIFE

PART II

TO SALONS AND STYLISTS

So how are you going to understand this client, cater so you will not lose her as a client?

Let's begin with understanding the PHYSIOLOGY AND STRUCTURES OF HAIR!

All this will be in laymen's terms for easy understanding

Understanding the basics goes a long way with many things and it's essential to understand this so you can see it for what it is.

WHAT ARE THESE DRUGS I AM TAKIN WHAT EFFECTS ARE THEY HAVING

Why not explain them to her if she comes across with any questions

That way you can understand how the drugs coincide with the cell destruction and the division of cells.

Help her understand 3 very important steps that I call the NEUTRALIZING SHAMPOO

Why is a nutrionist and naturopath so important?

Many times you will encounter a client who is very weak, nauseous will even be having severe migraines if she happens to show up for an appointment 2 to 3 days after her treatment, you will need to understand this without being judgmental!

And if she happens to come to your salon, 1 out of 10 is because she wants to feel normal and get on with her life!

You will play a big role with this and this where you will need to be patient!

HAIR LOSS PREVENTION DURING CHEMO IS IT POSSIBLE?

Have pamphlets of scalp cooling so at least she's aware of this possibility remember she will not be told everything and you can be a great source of information if you keep on top of these things so when your client does happen to come in you can give her a packet for her to read at her leisure.

MY SKIN IS DRY AND ACTING FUNNY

Her scalp may be irritable why not be able to explain it to her if she happens to ask these questions, more likely than not she will say part of her body is irritable from the treatment.

It is very important to be able to offer some part of service to her if your salon has spa services available.

Remember even if it's a little hand massage, bring relief to a little area goes a long way.

The importance of skin care is vital during this time, if she happens to come to cut all her hair off now's a good time to go over conditioning treatments for her that will sooth her scalp.

WHAT YOU NEED TO
UNDERSTAND

There are 3 stages of hair

ANAGEN: growth of hair

CATAGEN: degeneration of hair, during this stage the mitotic activity of the hair bulb ceases

TELOGEN: replacement (resting phase)

*MITOTIC: is the process of cell division in other words

MITOSIS (key definition when understanding what goes on with the cancer cells)

HAIR FOLLICLES: are developed during $3^{rd}/4^{th}$ month of pregnancy, a bud of closely patched cells forms in the DERMIS in a DISORGANISED FASHION there's very little attachment between the CELLS, they are constantly DIVIDING which adds to the confusion to an already CONGESTED SITUATION!

While in the epidermis another group of CELLS known as the HAIR GERM enlarges and extends downward into the DERMIS where it envelops the cluster of DERMAL CELLS.

The cluster of CELLS becomes the DERMAL PAPILLA without which:

THE HAIR WOULD NOT EXIST

The PAPILLA is the main communication LINK between the HAIR FOLLICE and the rest of the BODY.

(key when dealing with a client that doesn't want to discuss what's going on internally the hair will speak to you)

Most importantly the BLOOD passes through the PAPILLA by means of the CAPILLARIES.

As a result, the PAPILLA if affected by ALL imbalances of the body that are reflected in the BLOOD which in turn can AFFECT the HAIR FOLLICLE and HAIR.

*When studying to understand Trichology I became stuck with WNT SIGNALING which helps to regulate the follicle formation still trying to figure out if there was another explanation, so I decided to dig deeper since this part became a little confusing to me in truth it's nothing more than a dual function protein. Normal hair follicles rely on chemical communication between 2 basic CELL TYPES.

*modified keratinocytes: which form the outer skin epithelium

*modified fibroblasts: called DERMA PAPILLA CELLS

These 2 CELL groups must talk to each other through biochemical signals to ensure HAIR GROWTH and CYCLING OCCURS.

The CELLS must stay in close contact with each other to keep the process going.

I found this so interesting I kept digging deeper.

If you're a stylist that would like to further your studies and understanding in Disorders and Diseases of the Hair and Scalp please contact:

www.trichology.edu.au

apply for the Hair Practitioners Course is it complex YES is it DIFFICULT no you just need to have a desire to learn I just simplified it for you here and when you do choose to further your studies in *TRICHOLOGY* I highly advise you to invest in the ATLAS OF TRICHOLOGY and complete THE ENTIRE TRICHOLOGY COURSE , the 3 day course is worth it but THE FULL COURSE is simply AMAZING and can take you FURTHER. You would be able to serve your future and present clients so much better and will not regret it!

WNT SIGNALING EXPLANATION

PARACRINE: nearby cell communication, basic cell communication
AUTOCRINE: same cell communication
Which in turn is BETA' CATENIN a dual function protein regulating the coordination of cell to cell adhesion
MUTATION/OVER EXPRESSION OF B'CATENIN IS ASSOCIATED WITH MANY CANCERS

Come to find out *WNT SIGNALING-1ST IDENTIFIED for its role in CARCINOGENESIS actual formation of CANCER whereby normal CELLS are TRANSFORMED into
CANCER CELLS.
I found this part of my studies to be very interesting.

WHAT ARE CYTOSTATIC AND CYTOTOXIC DRUGS

As I started my journey in assisting clients with their new hair while dealing with cancer I started noticing that for each consultation they would let me in on what medication or therapy they were under. So here's a bit of advice at the end of the day I'm not an ONCOLOGIST so just listen to what they are telling you and do not become a doctor. However I became curious so I decided to look up the medications they were taking or therapies that were prescribed just so I can have a better understanding.

CYTOSTATIC: describes the way some anticancer drugs work

CYTOTOXIC: toxic to CELLS or CELL KILLING

So CHEMOTHERAPY is a CYTOTOXIC THERAPY

Then the other treatments do not aim to kill CANCER CELLS, they work by stopping the CANCER CELLS from MULTYPLYING so they stop the cancer from growing. This is:

CYTOSTATIC THERAPY

CYTOSTATIC: CELL STOPPING

CYTOTOXIC MEDICATION can affect ALL CELLS but it tends to affect:

CELLS THAT DIVIDE RAPIDLY or UNCONTROLLABLY

Example:

CANCEROUS CELLS

CELLS FROM THE GASTROINTESTINAL TRACT

reason why they will be complaining about loss of appetite

EARLY BLOOD CELLS IN THE BONE MARROW

And you guessed it

HAIR FOLLICLES

CYTOTOXIC AGENTS: cannot DISTINGUISH between NORMAL and MALIGNANT CELLS. Although normal CELLS have a greater capacity for repair.

CYTOTOXIC DRUGS ACT: by interfering with CELL DIVISION!

This is where ANAGEN EFFLUVIUM /TELEGEN EFFLUVIUM happens

This means OUTFLOW.

FREQUENTLY SEEN IN PEOPLE TAKING CYTOTOXIC DRUGS.

THREE IMPORTANT STEPS

Before I speak on this chapter I always compare these 3 steps in relation to the most important step after rinsing out a:

RELAXER OR PERM

If you do not open your eyes nor what's the important part of this service is, then you will lose. I always compare these 3 steps to:

NEUTRALIZING WHAT'S GOING ON

You might understand them separately but you must truly understand them collectively. These 3 are actually 1.

PAY ATTENTION, READ AND UNDERSTAND IT!
You'll get it look for the key words and they will speak to you!

THREE IMPORTANT THINGS TO UNDERSTAND
Ph balance Sugar Iodized Salt

IODIZED SALT/SODIUM CHLORIDE:

The beginning of all chronic diseases is marked by the loss of POTASSIUM from the cell and the invasion of SODIUM CHLORIDE.
the flavoring chemical compound that comprises SALT
Furthermore IODIZED SALT PROMOTES excessive cellular MITOSIS in other words CELL DIVISION

PROMOTES CANCER

CANCER: lives in an extremely ACIDIC ENVIORMENT and is DEVOID OF OXYGEN

ACIDOSIS: CREATES CANCER

The excess of ACIDIFICATION in the body is the cause of all DEGENERATIVE DISEASES when the balance is broken, the body starts to produce and store more ACIDIC and TOXIC WASTE it cannot handle. Which in turn MANIFEST VARIOUS AILMENTS.

CANCER LOVES SUGAR--SUGAR FEEDS CANCER

Because it is DEVOID OF OXYGEN: fermentation of sugar

Acidity in turn EXPELS OXYGEN FROM CELLS

The body does not run on SUGAR

So you have:

OBLIGATE AEROBE: organism that requires oxygen to grow

CANCER CELLS PARTIAL ANAEROBES: microorganism that can live and grow in the absence of OXYGEN

They're ANAEROBIC: living without air

When EATING SUGAR, think about your IMMUNE SYSTEM slowing down to a crawl.

SUGAR is devoid of minerals, vitamins, fiber and has such a deterioration on the;

ENDOCRINE SYSTEM

Major health organizations agree that SUGAR CONSUMPTION in AMERICA is the #1 of the 3 major causes of a DEGENERATIVE DISEASE.

*when we need VITAMIN C we crave SWEET FOODS. Eating lots of SUGAR and HIGH CHOLESTEROL FOODS FEED CANCER.

This is why we need more POTASSIUM in our diets.

POTASSIUM: is an ELECTROLYTE an assists in a range of essential body functions namely:

PH BALANCE

It all goes back to PH BALANCE

PH STRIPS can be purchased at any drug store you yourself can check for PH BALANCE

The PH is an INDICATOR/NOT A GOAL TO REACH, by maintaining the bodies PH BALANCE

YOU WILL PROTECT THE BODY

Healthy cells live in an ALKALINE ENVIORMENT

Meaning more ALKALINE FOODS, higher ALKALINE levels help discard WASTE AN TOXINS

ALKALINE ENVIORMENTS are less prone to cause CORROSION than ACIDIC ENVIORMENTS

CANCER CELLS CANNOT GROW IN AN ALKALINE ENVIORMENT

This is why I stress and it is important to guide your client to a NATURAPATHIC DOCTOR to work alongside her ONCOLOGIST.

*it is illegal in the U.S. To treat a patient that is under a doctor's care and living with cancer HOLISTICALLY.

WHERE AND HOW I WOULD COME IN AND ACCOMMODATE THE CLIENT

So what are you going to offer your clients and how are you going to help them?

Are you just going to be selling her a WIG or are you going to be helping her with NEW HAIR a NEW HAIRSTYLE as well as trying NEW COLORS?

Are you going to lift her up and get her to a place that she feels normal again?

What are you doing to better yourself, are you taking classes on wig styling, how to alter wigs and enhance them?

Or are you just offering her A WIG, so that she can be on her WAY?

Who are you going to be that day?

Remember she is still going home with a lot on her mind!

SO WHY NOT MAKE IT AN EXPERIENCE FOR HER

THE OUTBURSTS

From time to time you will experience some clients are just so angry they want to curse, you cannot take this personal it's just what they're going through and part of the stages . I for the most part allow them to be who they are; this is one of the reasons why they gravitate to me. I hold no judgmental attitude towards them.

I had a client who just came to buy a regular synthetic unit, since she didn't want to purchase a higher priced one. I had cut all her hair off, we were by ourselves of course so she was comfortable, I let her SCREAM, YELL AND CURSE she was venting her frustrations out not towards me but her situation and since I like to have somewhat of a sailors mouth at times, I joined as well in the fracas so she wouldn't be alone, since there was a couple of mofo's that needed to be told that day.

You need to let her vent it's not PERSONAL, we actually ended up having a great time, laughing hysterically and she was relieved.

I was also happy for her because her ANXIETY vanished and I was able to tell a couple of imaginary people where the hell to go.

Out of all of this, once she was comfortable with her NEW HAIR, she looked at me and said:

I look cute but do you think some biaaatch is going to look at me and say who the hell does she think she is with this new hair?

I hugged her kissed her and said it's time to go

SHE FELT LIKE HERSELF......................

THE SUPPORT SYSTEM

Things to consider and understand will be the support system that is coming with her. You need to be ahead of the game.

Be prepared mentally when this client makes an appointment with you they will either be arriving with someone or a group of people, for the most part up to 5 people.

Anything after 5 I start looking for a circus tent.

This can be very tricky and frustrating when consulting with her because psychologically something else is playing in the minds of the support system and what they are trying to do is carry the weight for her, actually to the point, not all but some that it's the end of the line for her!

I find this group rather ridiculous. You will find that when this client sits in your chair as the consultation has begun with her, immediately there is going to be a wave of questions that at times comes off as an attack!

Prepare yourself for there will be that one special person in the group that I lovingly call: THE SUPER HERO

Oh they will know everything even though she has come to see you they have been online all night to gather as much information as they can for her consultation, I just shake my head the main clown has entered the room!

Now remember she is coming to you for HELP, GUIDANCE AND ASSISTANCE on making a decision on new hair for her.

SO HOW DO I HANDLE THIS WORSE CASE SCENARIO

- When the client calls me I usually question if she's coming with someone, family or friends.
- I usually ask is she coming to consider cutting her hair off or to make a decision selecting hair.
- When she comes to the salon I ask her to take a seat in my chair and offer her something
- I usually will tell her give me a minute I am going to speak with the support system first!
- I make sure that she is not in the same room or within earshot from them, so she's not able to listen to what I have to tell them.
- I tell the support to please allow me to conduct the consultation without any interruption.
- If they have a need to ask a question just raise their hands without jumping out and asking them.
- I will REPRIMAND them that at NO TIME during this consultation NO ONE and I MEAN NO ONE, I
  FORBID IT is to start trying on wigs and playing with them in front of her.

9. DO YOU KNOW WHY? YOU ARE MOCKING HER!

She will begin to get ANGRY within you will not know it but she is, get frustrated, start feeling like it's a WASTE OF TIME and the biggest hint she will end up with an interesting smile on her face, more like a MONA LISA SMILE!

This is a clear indication that this consultation is about to be over and she will kindly say I will call you, the sale will most likely not happen reason being, for all you know it alls!

NO ONE WAS LISTENING TO HER AND SHE IS FRUSTRATED!

*If you are showing her samples of hair units make sure they are displayed on a HIGH SHELF. Then bring them down to try on 2 at a time don't make it confusing.

Ask her to bring a picture of what she would like her new hair to look like or a picture of herself if she just wants her old look back but make sure to see if she would like to add a couple of highlights to the unit she'll love them!

STORY TIME

One year a new client had come to the salon that had found me online. She also came with THE FRIEND! I already knew what to expect so it was no biggie and it always repeats itself. However this was the first time I experienced a full blown CLOWN ACT, that wasn't expected.

The client that I was consulting came in wearing a knitted cap on her head, had already started her treatment so it was a matter of time before she would start losing her hair.

I made the mistake to have some sample units on a table so they were at arm's length for me to show and explain them to her. Immediately the friend started with THE QUESTIONS not towards me but towards the client I started noticing how her friend's emotions started changing and her face became flustered.

Her friend had just started speaking to her in their language was flooding her with questions. Without her knowledge I somewhat understood everything she was asking her of me so I had just grinned, for the client had answered her in their language and said, he's very knowledgeable and knows what he's talking about so the friend responded, I'm not sure, YOU TRUST HIM, she said yes. After all this vacillating back and forth, I had asked the client to remove her cap, so I would be able to take measurements I figured her hair was short not knowing she had SHAVED IT ALL OFF.

I grabbed her hand and asked why she shaved it all off, she had told me: TO ALL STYLIST AND ANYONE CATERING TO THIS SPECIFIC CLIENT!

SHE WAS TAKING CONTROL OF THE SITUATION NOT YOU OR THE FRIEND

See she was letting you know ahead of time so you will not begin with the FOOLERY!

As I was taking her measurements, selecting quality of hair, matching color, density as well as texture. I really didn't have nothing to go by except her friend who was suspicious of me so I asked her would she compare it to hers if there was a choice she said yes color, length and texture wise she said yes, I said great I have a point of reference to work from.

IMMEDIATEDLY while I was reassuring the client and she was getting ready to sign the contract. THE FRIEND jumped directly in FRONT OF THE BOTH OF US, now picture this her friend has no hair on her head, her health is hanging in the balance, she's making this decision as well. This so called friend stood directly in front of the mirror turned around and had the nerve to ask.

HOW DOES THIS WIG LOOK ON ME?

With a head full of hair to begin with, I was actually shocked as was the client by then at this point I was expecting THE MONA LISA SMILE, she signed the contract. I hugged the client reassured her and I said give me a minute with your friend.

I took her friend into the back room and told her I think I know what I'm doing that wasn't necessary at all!

She in turn said she was going to get me if I was, I don't know bamboozling her, well since she threw that in my direction, I told her you have no clue what you just did and you're a woman, YOU HAVE MADE THIS ABOUT YOURSELF, not her.

Do you not realize that you have made her angry oh yes she's mad at you and you do not even know it, but she is, and you'll be driving home with her! Immediately she started crying and telling me she didn't want to lose her. Now look at who the hell I had to give strength to, I had hugged her and told her she's going to be okay now clean yourself up and be a friend.

The new hair arrives, this time the client came with her mother in law, she was only able to speak in her language, so here we go again, and I immediately started understanding everything they were saying.

This time was different though the client said wow this is better than how my own hair was, the color was just off by 1 level she was very happy and her mother in law was impressed. Coincidentally she had owned a wig salon and began asking her to ask me how I was able to

Get it to look like that? This is what we ended up talking about, the client was happy and there was no pressure.

When she was about to leave the client felt she had to apologize for the friends behavior the last time,

now your foolish behind also had to put this pressure on her as well IT'S NOT ABOUT YOU might as well start wearing a DUNCE CAP while carrying around ALL DAY SUCKER

I told her that was no big deal, you go live your life, GET IT AND ENJOY YOUR HAIR, I'm always encountering a CIRCUS ACT.

HUGGED HER, KISSED HER AND TOLD HER EVERYTHING WILL BE OKAY!

MORAL OF THE STORY:

DON'T LOOK LIKE A FOOL TRYING ON WIGS IN FRONT OF HER AGAIN ....
IT'S NOT ABOUT YOU AND IT NEVER WILL BE!
SO LETS TALK ABOUT THIS DECISION, BEING IN CONTROL

Once she is diagnosed with the doctor letting her know these are the results we have to follow steps 1-2 and 3.

Her mind will start racing, she has appointments that need to be met! She might be traveling for a business project she's working on, her children's schedules and the list can go on.

In her mind HOW AM I GOING TO JUGGLE ALL OF THIS, now this is added to the, to do list.

They actually enter a SHOCK PHASE who really wants to hear this! Many things will be outside of their control but they will strive to control the things they can, and one of them is I'M CUTTING/SHAVING all my hair off, BEFORE IT FALLS OFF.

SHE WANTS TO CONTROL IT!

This can also work in reverse as well.

STORY TIME

I'll do a two for 1, years ago I had a consultation with a very beautiful woman, we had spoken on the phone first prior to her visiting me. I guided her through the steps, explained how she wanted the hair color, density etc.

Her main concern she had requested was the hair was to be super short like a pixie. I had creative freedom no problem.

She signed the contract and handed me a cash deposit. The weeks passed, the unit came in beautiful as usual. I was ecstatic since I wanted to do that pixie cut.

I must have called her 7 to 8 time to come and receive her new hair.

She never responded nor did I hear from her, finally after 2 or 3 months after that I finally got a hold of her, I had asked what had happened, she told me it wasn't necessary for her to have the new hair she decided to ROCK A BALDIE!

I said oh ok! I was a bit confused no one just leaves me a cash deposit nor pick up their hair. She said don't worry about it that's for your troubles!

This was her way of CONTROLLING THE SITUATION and LIVING HER LIFE!

See the cancer became NON'EXISTANT to her.

One 4th of July years later I had run into her on the west side highway in NYC, she happened to be happily walking with her family and was vibrant, she introduced me to her husband and smiled.

I couldn't believe I had run into her, I chuckled and said:

I still have your hair...........her response: I DON'T NEED IT.

(2)

Now my flamed hair client never shaved or cut her hair real short she instead chose to hold on to her hair for as long as possible.

She had called me one day and said OZZY, I think it's time to cut my hair short, but I do not want you to see me like this. I'm so use to this that it is practically seems normal to me.

She had come in sat took her hair off and I needed not cut it, she was a bit embarrassed. I practically combed all of her hair off and cutting it wasn't necessary. This was her way of CONTROLLING the situation.

I washed her scalp afterwards, she put her hair back on and when I would see her from then on she would not allow me to see her without her hair and that was ok.

SHE CONTROLLED IT THIS WAY.............................
LET THEM HAVE CONTROL YOU DON'T CHOOSE FOR THEM!

BE CAREFUL HOW
YOU ADVERTISE

What is this that I am looking at! A client will be very perceptive of all that is going on in the room. If you're going to market your business and strategically trying to promote the product make sure what she is looking at makes sense to her!

Example: I knew of someone who posted photos of a client showing results of what was achieved with before and after pictures. Not sure where the person was going with this I looked at the photos that were posted.

The pictures consisted of a young model if I'm exaggerating maybe 25 years old, ordinary girl not a classic beauty and if this is the case our job as beauty professionals is to bring that out of her.

The first pictures were the client with her problem area that was sparse and fine, the photo should have been cropped with the problem area highlighted.

The second set of photos of the results were of the problem area tufted with the sides of the hair combed up in a form of a messy chignon

Furthermore since the client was a candidate for additional hair the enhancement that was placed on her which appeared to be more plopped was a typical style some older woman from the mid 70's or early *80's would've worn.

I looked at these photos and said wow. This poor girl agreed to do this not sure there was even a consensual signed agreement has her face plastered on this site with before and after pictures had somewhat of a beginning and a unwanted end!

The result was a horrible marketing strategy let me do this and off you go!

So I decided to run a test with a client of mine. I had asked her to give me her opinion with these photos, If you were a client with this problem, came across these photos on this site what would your feeling be?

She answered:

1. I see her but what is all that around her? (The salon was a mess!)
2. Ok I see what the problem is but this other picture is actually HIDING THE RESULTS it looks like they're hiding something or there isn't any real results, as if the stylist is being DECEPTIVE!
3. This is the AFTER that's the best they could do? I wouldn't go there!

1st we'll begin with she was no classic beauty our jobs regardless of the client is to bring that out of her if she doesn't feel or see herself like that, we are in the BEAUTY INDUSTRY!

Have a very clear photo of what you are trying to explain with a polished result so the future client can process the information to make an intelligent decision meaning if it's hair breakage and growth of hair, hair should be washed, combed out so you can realistically see the results, not tied up in a bunch so it seems like a lot of hair grew. This is considered deceptive marketing.

Photos should not include anything else in them specifically a salon in disarray with garbage all about.

4. The results a final picture especially if it's additional hair should not end up looking like a leftover washed up 70's early 80's person with a horrible do.

This should be polished and executed perfectly it shouldn't resonate I needed this photo for a marketing campaign so I can get clients!

This came through the models face in the photo, a very poor strategic move, even though I'm sure this was done more for a favor than an actual consumer her photo said DON'T COME!

This is not how you want your outcome to be!

Same goes for the salon the client is looking at everything and is observant.

ADVICE FOR STYLIST GETTING INTO CUSTOM DESIGN

So how are you going to listen to this client when she has a specific request?

For example: OPRAH'S HAIRSTYLE, BRIDGETTE BARDOT, MARILYN MONROE, I WANT LONG THICK HAIR, ANNETTE FUNICELLO, MARIA CALLAS, LOLLOBRIGIDA trust me all these women sat in my chair so get ready they will be in yours as well.

And yes they will be some asking for these specific requests, so you will need to be very careful how you will listen to them.

Take into consideration HOW SHE IS SEEING THINGS:

For example If they consider OPRAH'S HAIRSTYLE, especially the curly one.

The client is not specifically asking for all that hair, in truth she wants that look, in a way that would complement her facial structure and lifestyle, and she most likely will want it cut above her shoulder framed around her face with minimal density.

YOUR MIND IS REGISTRING: ALL OF THIS HAIR, I'm going to give it to her long thick super curly WOW! This is going to be great.

When you end up crowning her with this look that she requested she's going to look in the mirror and say wow that's a lot of hair, I'm not sure.

I promise you everything will go downhill from there. IT WILL OVERWHELM HER.

The key to all of this is that she is looking at herself, not 2 DIFFERENT PEOPLE.

If she picks her hair up on Monday by Thursday OPRAH and her will be in a side alley having a knocked out drag down fight and she will not wear the hair! She would have kicked her behind.

I want LONG THICK HAIR: density plays a big role here, the hair can be long but in truth she's asking for the richness of the color that makes it look thick.

I want to look like MARILYN MONROE, she doesn't necessarily want those flips and dips, it's the color she's requesting.

And the list goes on and on, you must be very careful how you are listening to the clients.

What may sound reasonable to you might register differently to her! SO DON'T FORGET IT………

Well here I am back at star bucks in Bloomfield NJ drinking my favorite (very berry hibiscus trenti tea).

I had just signed the lease to my new salon in Montclair, NJ. This will be my 3rd salon WTH did I just sign, now to relocate, I hate moving since I like to remain stable and in one location. There's always so much ruckus when moving but I guess I'm use to the chaos and craziness.

So in order for me to move forward with all that's going to come my way, I needed to be at the ground level and be a storefront again.

The new space is great is what' I've wanted and desiring for the 1st time in a very long time I will have someone else working alongside me. We'll get along fine I'm so in tune with women and understand them. So it'll be great.

The best part of this move, the new space has a section that I have desired, A PRIVATE ROOM! Which is essential when catering to any hair loss client, so I'm super excited because of my other girls can be about their business in the front of the salon and I'll still be by myself in my PRIVATE ROOM with my client.

It was meant for me, ever since my good friend MARILYN had told me a year earlier, she had said OZZY you have to check this space out it has your name all over it, especially THE PRIVATE ROOM. It's meant for you, so for a whole year and ½ I would be going around getting to know the landlord so she could become familiar with me.

What I was doing was CLAIMING IT and making it mine in my mind as well as envisioning myself in the space.

I'm still pinching myself every time I do this. 2016 is going to be an incredible year for me and I have to be ready to walk in his PROMISES and into my DESTINY!

I'm so grateful and humble at this moment! Marilyn and I can finally be together as we were meant to be, there was only one person missing our 3rd wheel ROBYN who transitioned 3 yrs. prior. So this is for your memory ROBYN.

Ever since we met at my old space 12 years ago it was meant for us to be together we had instantly clicked.

So I'm dedicating this chapter to MARILYN

For dealing with all my CRAZY ANTICS (WHAT)

Btw what fabulous restaurant are we going to after work on Saturday? SMILE.........

BE CAREFUL HOW YOU TREAT SOMEONE, IT'S NOT ALWAYS ABOUT YOU!

Once you begin thinking about putting yourself in that person shoes this will make total sense to you.

It is important to understand her FEELINGS and EMOTIONS regardless if she's expressing them.

We all have problems and are frustrated, many are a paycheck away from being homeless, and tragedy can happen you never know when it's going to come knocking at your door!

PERFECT EXAMPLE ....STORY TIME

One year I was working at a BRIDAL EXPO what a better place to be seen at promoting my business. The tables were set and of course I was the only one there with ADDITIONAL HAIR. I was discretely marketing this in a public forum.

Of course many women inquired asked questions and were curious.

All of a sudden BRIDEZILLA shows up hair down her back acting like a TOTAL BUFFOON!

There were about 3 or 4 in her group. Now remember when you start involving yourself in additional hair, studying hair loss and hair replacement, you will immediately start noticing many women with hair issues, things that you never even had bothered to look at or notice.

It was THE BUFFOON BRIDE and the other women, I've experienced so much in this hair world that I can point out the one that's totally trying to hide and be part of the group.

One of the ladies in the group was discretely trying to gather up information from the table that was laid out even though her hair was long past her shoulders.

Around this time I immediately noticed the TENSION, ANXIETY and the PRESSURE. You see her hair was styled with a comb over; she purposely styled it that way.

She had major diffused hair loss in the front and the very top, so I approached her quietly, smiled looked her in the eyes and said if you have any questions take the information call me at the salon and I will answer any of this for you.

Now the BUFFOON BRIDE immediately yelled out I DON'T HAVE ANY NEED FOR THAT I HAVE LONG BEAUTIFUL HAIR for my wedding.

AGAIN ....IT'S NOT ABOUT YOU so please keep that in mind SMDH

BUFFOON your wedding was a year away and many things can happen from the time you INSULTED YOUR FRIEND to that INCONSEQUENTIAL WEDDING. The result with what I was trying to discretely help her friend with was just shot down.

Yes I was promoting/marketing my business at this bridal expo. Now listen very carefully if you happen to see me at any of these events and I'm specifically talking to you that get besides themselves with these character traits. You are not who I'm looking for unless you are living with this condition.

1. I'm right where I need to be
2. All the women are interested and have questions.
3. The women are gathering my info each one knows one! Remember that.
4. The special person I'm looking for is a needs based client not a want. I was in a perfect arena!
5. BUFFOON automatically thought I was for her; again IT'S NOT ABOUT YOU!

Now if you ever encounter me out and about promoting my business, it's best to ask about the information before being BOISTEROUS, CANTANKEROUS and end up HUMILIATING the person whose with you. It's not always you who is looking for me.

I wouldn't have been surprised if the woman with the hair problem ended up sleeping with the friend's fiancé the night before the wedding just to pay her back.

This is why it's important to be UNDERSTANDING AND SENSITIVE.........

WITH A FRIEND LIKE THAT WHO NEEDS AN ENEMY

WHY IS IT I HAVE TO BE PATIENT

I'm only going to sell her some hair.

NOT QUITE! One main thing that you need to do is REASSURE your client during this consultation and make her as comfortable as possible!

If this is a person who has never worn additional hair it is best to have at least 4 different sample units that she can try on, you will need to definitely set aside some time for her.

In the beginning of this journey I didn't understand this. I was having full blown conversations in my head (WTH) is taking so long? It's just hair!

NO IT'S NOT JUST HAIR IT'S HER LIFE and how she's going to MOVE ON with it.

If she has already been diagnosed and has called you, I highly advise you to make this fun for her. Realizing this is NEW TO HER.

It's going to be frightening, confusing as well as daunting she's not exactly sure what's she's looking for!

SHE HAS JUST BEEN GIVEN HER DEADLINE!

She most likely is going to want something that resembles her!

You need to become familiar with all types of hair units so it can register with you and you will be able to explain it to her, in a clear and understandable way.

You will also need to give her options she might not be able to afford the Mercedes truck but will be able to afford the Ford focus.

So here's what I do and it works out perfectly basically all the time.

Since one of the side effects of the treatments might be discoloration of the skin:

- Would you like to try highlights on just to add a splash of color? Oh you should try this and since you're going to be a new person, why not some color just a little, that way it will brighten your face.
- Would you like to try a shorter layered style, you should.
- Why not ask her what has always been her dream hairstyle that's she's been thinking about. GO FOR IT. It's a new you and it's only TEMPORARY.
- Have a long hair unit, mid length unit, short and super short unit. Let her try them all on at least once.

Begin with the shortest one so she can envision herself BRAND NEW and then work your way up to normalcy.

If you are not going to be a hair replacement specialist and this is not for everyone even if they think it is it's not, because there will be many and I mean many what I like to call (OH SHIT MOMENTS), however I have conquered this, it took a minute but I figured it out . Things have a way of repeating themselves.

You will need to be on top of your game! If you're going to be a specialist on custom design you definitely need to know your audience because it will most definitely be a MELTING POT. You cannot be JUDGEMENTAL about either.

She will know it and see through your smile if that's how you will approach it.

There a many companies you can open accounts with that carry beautiful high fiber synthetic hair in a variety of styles. This will most likely be your best bet a make it a bit easier for you to do deal with.

You also need to be aware that the base of the unit might be itchy to some. So it's best to always use A WIG LINER when trying on or wearing the unit or she might just be comfortable without it as well. It's an Individual preference.

This is why it's very important to understand wig bases and become familiar with them.

When you have conquered these little techniques the consultation will run much smoother and not as long!

A word of advice:

SHE WANTS TO BE LISTENED TO!!!!!!!!!!!!!!!!!!!!!

Not the other way around so if you make the answers easier for her and know them ahead of time.

SHE WILL REGISTER IT AS BEING LISTENED TO, BE IMPRESSED, HAVE A HUGE SMILE, AND WILL NOT SERVE YOU THE MONA LISA SMILE…..

LISTEN TO YOUR CLIENTS WITH NO WORDS BEING EXCHANGED

When you are allowing your client to try on the hair units and different styles DO NOT and I mean this from a place of knowledge and understanding, if she asks you how does this look on me at no time immediately complement her nor patronize her. THIS IS NEW TO HER. As stated earlier let and help her find the comfort level and sense of normalcy.

THIS REQUIRES A LOT OF PATIENCE, I've conquered this to a point it has become a short fun experience for the both of us.

If you begin with it looks good on you, oh that looks good, you should get it, it's not that bad, and you're good to go.

This goes for the so called SUPPORT SYSTEM as well.

IT'S NOT ABOUT YOU! YOU CHOSE TO HELP HER OUT.

With all that being said, are you able to see, understand, how unattached and pressured that sale will feel to her if you do not become involved with how she is feeling.

SHE'S NOT STUPID: THE MONA LISA SMILE will appear and everything will be over, she will rather go without, since you have become part of her FRUSTRATION and she will BE ANGRY!

*take yourself out, make it fun, help her decide and definitely do not put the hair on yourself, you help her put it on!

She's going to be NERVOUS in the beginning so expect this.

This is why these steps are essential.

One thing she will be doing a lot of once the unit/new hair is on; she will be fidgeting with it. DO NOT immediately go try and adjust it comb or style it for her! The key here is to listen to what she is saying without actually anything being said.

Observe her actions in the mirror she will let you know exactly what she wants, all you will need to do is listen in SILENCE and be able to have an answer.

- What she is indirectly telling you is: how are others going to perceive me so they will not pay attention to this.
- Is this hair manageable / versatile enough that I can run my fingers through it, have it somewhat messy, but styled the way I like it, so it feels normal to me.
- If you complement her while she's doing this in the mirror, it's going to register as if I'm being rushed to get this and get out of here! PATIENCE IS A REQUIREMENT allow her space. If you do this she'll respond with this hair is not bad at all, I'm sure I'll be able to adjust and wear her comfortably and not be so concerned. THE NEW ME.
- Give her THE SPACE, LISTEN AND BE PATIENT
- Again offer different options before any of this, she'll be very happy and love you for it.

THE SCALE OF THE PROBLEM...
SECRET SUFFERING

Take into consideration how she is dealing with this hair loss though it is through chemo or an auto immune disorder

- THE END OF YOUTH AND GETTING OLDER
- INABILITY TO STYLE HAIR
- DISSATISFACTION WITH APPEARANCE AND BODY IMAGE
- LOSS OF PERSONAL ATTRACTIVENESS AND FEAR OF NOT LOOKING ATTRACTIVE TO OTHERS.
- LOW SELF ESTEEEM
- EMBARRASSMENT, LOSS OF CONFIDENCE, SHYNESS
- SOCIAL TEASIN AND HUMILIATION
- FEELINGS OF DEPRESSION AND INTROVERSION
- LOSING SOMETHING ABOUT CONTROL OF THEIR LIFE, HAVE HIGHER LEVELS OF ANXIETY & DEPRESSION.
- SUBCONSCIOUS EMOTIONS: ENVY & JEALOUSY EVERYONE ELSE HAS PERFECT HAIR.
- WORK RELATED PROBLEMS
- NEGATIVE EFFECTS ON SOCIAL LIFE: upon meeting someone, one of the first things you notice is their hair.
- START EXCERCISING TO IMPROVE PHYSIQUE
- WEAR HATS OR CAPS EVEN IN WARM WEATHER
- DRESS NICER

40% of women with hair loss or alopecia have marital problems
63% claim to have career related problems

PSYCHOSOMATIC ISSUES
AND HOW SHE FEELS

One time a client of mine and I had a one on one, she was happy her hair had come back and had asked me about what products to use on her hair after I shaped it up for her.

She didn't want much cut off since it had grown back, after this we sat and chatted. She looked great and healthy again a year had passed since her trial living with cancer. What was interesting to me was her focus on having repercussion and cancer coming back to attack her, you will need to understand this is another symptom and feeling that will be going on in her mind when she visits you.

She went on to say that in the beginning of wearing her new hair and trying to adjust to it, that she would open her front door look both ways to see if anyone was looking and go about her business, another symptom. She felt and would feel as if she is the only one even though so many wear additional hair as a fashion statement.

Even more interesting is when this person would be complemented on her looks, she felt like she was living a lie dreading and fearing if it was going to RETURN!

This client tickled me after all this telling me how she got so accustomed to wearing her new hair that she didn't know what to do with her own hair so we both started chuckling.

See she and the new hair had become one person throughout her trial period.

In addition to this when this client had walked in, it just so happened that I was working on a unit that another client had left for me to spruce up. You see this was perfect timing, I did not know that she was going to speak to me about THE FEAR OF REPURCUSSION!

Actually the unit that I was working on was for a client that was going through the process all over again. So she had asked me what I was doing with the unit. So I explained it to her.

NOW LISTEN CAREFULLY CHILDREN

If you understand wig making and have taken courses especially on ventilation which I am able to do and teach. REMEMBER THERE ARE NO RULES! Ventilating is the art of inserting hair with a very fine needle to a net much like a latch Hook rug but on a very fine scale. I love doing this it is rather relaxing to me.

Now here's a key to helping out the other client you see she was going through this again, I had taken care of the unit, razor cut the front to make it look softer so she would be able to spike it up if she wanted to. The unit was a rather mousy medium brown with some muted highlights, when I had placed it on her head, even though she liked the cut and how I had styled it, I suggested it would need a little bit of color just to brighten her up!

She agreed and was happy that I had offered, she in turn asked me what the cost would be?

I DIDN'T TELL HER SHE ASKED ME.....BIG DIFFERENCE

The client is very aware that she is going to purchase something so do not make this mistake. Now the reason I advised on that is because this was the old hair from the first time and I wanted for her to see a NEW HER not the OLD ONE! That way she will be more focused on how cute her hair looks than leaving my salon saying I'M GOING THROUGH THIS AGAIN and leaving. She will not be thinking about that at all, all that she will be focusing on is that she is cute, and this is how you want her to feel!

If you are a stylist who is not a custom wig maker/custom designer you can be creative. Take cut wefts of hair attach or sew them throughout the unit and just add your personal touch......THEY'LL LOVE IT and above all this THERE ARE NO RULES.

BE CREATIVE, BE DIFFERENT AND STAND OUT

One of my greatest feelings is helping out a client that had known me since my inception in the hair world, and assisting the owner. Not in a million years would I have thought that I would be sitting in her kitchen helping her out years later! The big story is she really knew me when and saw who I became. And if I would never had taken the risk to educate myself, I would not have been able to guide her and her 2 adult children when it was time to crown her with her new hair.

This feeling is indescribable; it was as if I was back in the kitchen with my aunt when I sat on her lap!

*this is for your memory MARY I'm glad to have known such a wonderful person.

ADDITIONAL ADVICE
FOR STYLISTS

When she comes to visit you for the consultation DO NOT BEGIN with:

OH I'M SO SORRY FOR WHAT'S HAPPENED

I DON'T KNOW WHAT TO SAY

ESPECIALLY WITH ALL THIS UNNEEDED CRYING!

SHE IS NOT DEAD! This is a living breathing person that has come to get her HAIR DONE and has trust in you!

A majority of these clients are referred to me. So they basically are at ease when meeting with me because of my reputation, history, especially my story.

So I begin with HEY HOW ARE YOU? COME IN

LET ME SEE AND HEAR WHAT'S GOING ON, see the difference.

Since I didn't begin with the BUFFOONERY, she will most likely open up and say I can't believe I'm going through this again, or this is my first, I really wasn't expecting this.

If you're reading this little tidbit you can make out the ease and there's no stress involved.

I also do not have the tolerance for the immediate crying from the person she is trusting to help her. I do not incorporate crying, I incorporate POSITIVE SPEAKING that does not even entail what she's going through.

She is there to get her HAIR DONE, that's it!

I've witnessed all this unnecessary crying from these stylists in the past and they look utterly RIDICULOUS!

AGAIN IT'S NOT ABOUT YOU…………………………..

And if you don't believe me look at your clients FACE, the MONA

LISA SMILE will appear, she will also be going to have this look like (WTF) am I doing here and what did I get myself into?

So begin with a HUGE SMILE, ENCOURAGE HER. OOOH let's see what we're going to select today!

AND REPEAT: If you are a woman, MODEL one of the hair units, please do not say HOW DOES THIS WIG LOOK ON ME? I SELECTED IT FOR YOU......... HELL NO!

Here's what you'll say instead:

I've tried this on so you can see what it would look like and maybe, you'll like it. It's just a point of reference so it can make sense to you by the way I wore this one with a little bit of color just to see the difference.

So let's begin selecting what you would like and what will work with your lifestyle, that way you can knock everyone out with your new look and hairstyle.

SELECT YOUR WORDS CAREFULLY

Many stylist can follow this same advice without wearing the hair, have an assistant or friend model the hair for her, WE ARE AT A FASHION SHOW.

It will connect, trust me and it will be fun.

You the stylist are meant to be creative and inspiring. NOT SCHEDULING A FUNERAL SALE AND GOODBYE!

BECAUSE THAT'S WHAT IT WILL BE GOOD BYE!

You will get a good reputation and clients will come and refer other clients to you as well

WHAT THE HELL IS SHE WEARING ON HER HEAD

From time to time I do encounter some very interesting clients, and yes this client is coming so you better be ready for her and be careful NOT TO JUDGE HER.

They will call make an appointment, she will not say anything on the phone, however when she does come, she's already wearing a unit that is torn up from the floor up.

A TOTAL DISASTER, it seems as if the APOCALYPSE has come and gone so more like a POSTAPOCALYPTIC look.

I had to get use to this years ago, it was shocking at first. I made the mistake of looking at the weapon of mass destruction that she was wearing.

It's one of those dull matted worn out units.

So here's a bit of advice because SHE IS COMING!

Upon the client coming to see me I make sure I stay focused on her eyes and look directly at her. She will immediately put her wall up and will reconsider if she should stay. If you make her comfortable she will instantly open up!

So it's best to focus on her eyes, welcome her in even though your thoughts are operating differently thinking (seriously what the hell is that?)

I start talking, looking into the mirror at her then I'll just sit down so I'm not over her, I'll ask her what would she like?

She will start laughing and tell you, I know this looks bad, you might be able to help me.

For the most part this specific client is trapped in a happy time in her life that's why the unit looks like that, she actually wants it FROZEN.

So we find a happy medium together key word: TOGETHER

The flip side to this she doesn't have to be bothered, it's so matted that in her eyes the hair is perfectly styled and this is how she's looking at it.

Once she's at ease, I kind of figure out what she wants and make it happen for her. She's ecstatic, disappears then comes back months and I mean months later.

But like the show HOARDERS she's back at it again, but the difference is I GAINED HER TRUST so they usually will call laughing because they know I'm going to get on their case.

In truth this client that I haven't passed judgment on has become the most LOYAL OF CLIENTS, MONEY IS neither OBJECT nor a PROBLEM! Boy do they have you fooled.

You should also consider NOT PROMISING HER THE WORLD and DEFINITELY DO NOT START QOUTING PRICES, for example.

This is going to be such and such dollars. You do not have to make her aware she's buying something, she already knows and has come fully loaded and prepared!

I usually wait till she'll ask that of me first and we'll make a selection together.

If it's a custom designed unit (example)

This will cost such and such dollars I require 1/2 of a deposit to commence with the job and agree with a contract.

If it's a synthetic wig: depending on what we selected together the price ranges from such and such to this because how it's constructed.

If you showing her units start shooting from that mouth about how much something costs, YOU WILL LOSE HER!

And this is how she is thinking: oh they just want my money and if she decides to buy from you, this is how you left her! And you will know it for she will give you THE MONA LISA SMILE.

Again she knows she has to pay for something, key word:

AGAIN

I for the most part give all my clients HUGS, KISSES make sure I look into their eyes even if she doesn't know me.

MAKE THAT EMOTIONAL CONNECTION.

Take into consideration this is a very deep emotional time for her, she has a' lot on her plate for the most part she might not be receiving this at home or from her spouse *we'll get to the husband in a few, he got it coming as well*

I have clients literally breakdown in my chest because they are scared and no one is REALLY LISTENING! So put yourself in their shoes.

Thank GOD, I have this gorgeous solid body so they can sulk in it. I feel like I'm reenacting a scene from CAT ON A HOT TIN ROOF when LIZ TAYLOR throws herself into PAUL NEWMANS ARMS .... (Chuckle)

Even when they do this I reassure them. It's going to be ok and I have made it fun for her. This also goes for my regular hair loss clients.

WHY IT'S NOT WORKING FOR ME

I remember sitting at a table with a certain individual at one of the conferences that I had attended. Take into consideration we are at a HAIR LOSS CONFERENCE with the TRICHOLOGY ASSOCIATION.

I find it very interesting that even though we are learning methods, treatments etc. for hair loss. Many are not involved in additional hair or have incorporated it into their business!

So here I am and one of the guests at the table brought up the subject on where they would be able to find reasonably priced wigs. So we started talking and the person really wasn't clear with what they were saying, I had asked them what are they specifically looking for, who are your clients, do you know them and are you already involved in selling hair?

THEIR RESPONSE: not many of the clients are purchasing from them, I find it difficult an *these clients* are not going to pay so much for hair. They cannot afford that! I've tried it and it just didn't work. As well as she finds the clients difficult and picky!

Now this is a woman and she had spoken TOTAL DEFEAT TO HER BUSINESS!

HOW ARE YOU GOING TO CATER TO A CLIENT IF YOU HAVE ALREADY:

- PASSED JUDGMENT
- YOU FOUND IT DIFFICULT
- THEY ARE NOT GOING TO PAY THAT MUCH
- IT DIDN'T WORK FOR HER
- THE CLIENTS PICKY FUSSY AND DIFFICULT

So let me break this down for you in layman's terms!

- THERE WAS ABSOLUTELY NO PATIENCE THERE
- THEY WERE NOT LISTENING TO HER CLIENTS REQUEST
- THEY WERE ALREADY JUDGING THEIR WALLETS WITH THEIR APPEARANCE......VERY BAD MOVE!
- THEY WANTED TO MAKE A QUICK TRANSACTION AND GET THE HELL OUT!

I was surprised because there was another thing missing:
THEY DID NOT MEET THEM AT AN EMOTIONAL LEVEL NOR DID THEY CARE TO LISTEN

I would've made that sale in 15 minutes.

I highly advise anyone, this person or any other person that happens to think like this to read:

MARKETING TO WOMEN by MARTI BARLETTA

Now if I have to recommend this to a female there's a serious problem!

One thing a woman in the hair loss field that is able to do, that I am not is wear a different styled unit every day if she wants, just so the client can connect when she comes in and become comfortable.

If she sees you wearing hair and making it fun she'll be at ease and buy it!

If I was to be wearing it, it would register as if I'm mocking her.

DO NOT COUNT THE MONEY IN THE CLIENTS WALLET!

She is coming to you for a service and she trusts you. This is not a DUMP and GO DATE.

If you overlook that, they might surprise you; this is why your tone has to be very clear and not rushed.

She knows YOU'RE JUDGING HER!

You'll look stupid and she'll give you THE MONA LISA SMILE.

DON'T RUSH HER AT ALL

This is why it's essential to a least have some sort of consultation over the phone before she comes to see you. This will make it all so much easier.

THE CLIENT WHO'S NOT THERE AND THE ONE WHO'S OVERJOYED

From time to time you will encounter this specific client, she'll come to you not all the time but once in a while so be expecting her, and please pay very close attention as well.

This client is in a BLANK STATE OF SHOCK, it's the only way I can describe her. It took me a minute to figure this one out.

So here's a little STORY:

Usually the clients that are referred to me or find me online are somewhat relieved since I am able to answer their questions. For some reason this client I couldn't so much. I met with her she had just been diagnosed with cancer; I started by standing in back of her, looking directly at her. I preceded with usual consultation explained to her the steps that needed to be taken and had given her options.

Actually this client was FROZEN through our time together, so this is what I noticed:

- It was as if she wasn't in the room with me.
- As I was talking to her she never made eye contact with me.
- She stopped looking in the mirror and proceeded to just stare at THE WALL the entire time.

I never said anything because I had to dig deeper, so I decided to turn the chair around, sit down and just be quiet, come to find out. It was her 4 children she was concerned about! So instead of discussing hair I discussed her children to reassure her that it was going to be ok.

I never experienced this trait before; I'm not sure what the doctors had told her or how they treated her that day. From my point of view her entire being stated to me THAT IT WAS OVER and she wasn't going to see her children again!

This is why she kept looking at the wall. Her life was in the balance, so she thought. No sale of hair was made that day it was very quiet and solemn. I'm not even sure what became of her after that. I just made sure to let her know I was available if she started treatment and needed hair. It was one of the most distant meetings I had ever encountered.

So sometime we just need to be a listening ear to someone.

On the FLIP SIDE:

One client came in went through the necessary steps, I designed the unit she wanted, explained the turnaround time etc. She was a very good sport with the whole experience, she had come right when the treatment was taking effect on her hair, and I had given her the fantasy hair cut she had been wanting since it was going to come off anyway.

It actually had come out better than I even expected, I also had added some funky highlights for effect. A week later after the cut it all came off, luckily her new hair with highlights came in exactly like her original hair, passed the shoulders layered with curls when I crowned her with it she couldn't believe it.

Before I had done any of this she was laying in my shampoo bowl wiped out with a full blown MIGRAINE that was kicking her butt in an out of sleep while I styled her hair on the mannequin. This was one of the side effects from the drugs.

I let her sleep, and then told her it was time to put her hair on. She was so happy and ecstatic. I guess the migraine mysteriously disappeared because we ended up having a RED HOT CAMERA SESSION; this was actually hysterical to me.

She was swinging her hair hugging me make her sister take numerous pictures of us together and went home super happy!

I promise you there will be experiences of HIGHS AND LOWS and you must be prepared for them.

Many times for all the clients that ends up buying new hair from me. ALWAYS and I mean ALWAYS they will end up taking pictures with me.

So be ready to expect the same regardless if it's the chemo client or any hair loss client. IT'S GOING TO OCCUR even if you look like a HOT WRECK from working all day... they want that HAPPY PICTURE.

BE READY FOR YOUR CLOSE UP BECAUSE IT'S COMING!

SO WHAT IS OZZY'S MAGIC FORMULA

Rule of thumb: BE YOURSELF

I get involved with the community and there are times I just do things for free, at least twice a year. I will speak to a group of women, nothing long, lengthy and drawn out. For the most part they want to listen to my personal story and I have one I just told you. So this should have a personal touch.

I reach out to other stylist who in turn reaches out to me because in truth they do not really understand this specific client. I have specific business cards that they hold at their stations. Take into consideration I am not your typical stylist, I have a much defined skill set and I make sure they are aware of it.

For the most part my regular clients talk about me and everyone knows someone who is affected whether it be regular hair loss or chemo client.

The mail man, the supply reps, beauty supply store every business imaginable.

For example and TRUE STORY:

The FED EX GUY: he was delivering packages to another business a town away since I'm always hyped up about what I do (not bragging about it) he was curious about what I was doing so are all the others that walk through my door.

EVERYONE KNOWS ONE:

Back to the story he encounters the receptionists at the other business they are friendly so she trusts him with her secret. He

Lets her know oh I know someone that's all he does and he's good you should check him out.

This woman has been my client for the last 7/8 years and is always stepping out looking fabulous.

This is a very easy simple and free marketing tool, so use it!

WORDS OF ENCOURAGEMENT
FOR STYLIST

It's funny I never thought about this part of my journey and how it was going to evolve. I'm very comfortable with this specific clientele. I do not need to worry about being THE BEST STYLIST nor be in the IN CROWD.

I AM THE IN and always HAVE BEEN.

I'm not your so called FABULOUS STYLIST worrying about being in the click with the rest. I've always wanted to STAND OUT and have STOOD OUT!

This specific clientele which is dealing, living with hair loss all across the board makes me feel different in a way that I feel that I'm on top of the world when they look at themselves, with their self-esteems soaring. I feel like I have given them back their lives. There is no explanation on this feeling or reaction.

I've been to so many hair shows and even though they are enjoyable, they have always left me with WHAT'S NEXT, I'M BORED! I've always liked a challenge and dealt with it head on. This truly excites me since I am able to express my creative side.

I'm here sitting in my kitchen staring up at a framed picture of my late grandmother in her kitchen cooking looking down at me with a smile, its right over the entry way, I'm wondering what is she saying to me through that photo.

This book even though I had written it, DID NOT COME EASY it was rather cathartic / therapeutic and helpful to me, it did open some wounds. But if not for those wounds I would not had been able to move forward and onward to be able to help someone out.

I encourage you to challenge yourself like I have. You need not be with the group, let the group come to you this has always been my motto. They worry about groups not me. I AM THE GROUP AND CLICK you want to be with.

It's better for someone to know you than you know them! For it's not who I know, it's who knows me.

Many and I mean many stylist try and want to emulate me it all comes back to me why because they can't it's not the same, it's not coming from a place that is not given to them.

I am not the stylist at the hair show looking for attention because they are so grand. They actually bore me, I start questioning them in my mind and end up seeing them for who they are LIFELESS.

WHAT ARE YOU TRULY OFFERING TO MAKE A DIFFERENCE AND STAND OUT?

This walk will be alone but there'll be a second set of footprints walking alongside you, if you just believe. You just read my story if I had never stepped out and taken the necessary steps to proceed in this walk I would have never known, not in a million years I would have thought I would be asked to speak at a conference in front of numerous people, different venues or groups of women, create a fundraiser and raise the money, have been interviewed on radio music channel, write a lecture, be filmed for a documentary just imagine if I would had said no to the lady who introduced me into this hair additions world and if I didn't invest in my career think about it, I would not have been able to help numerous clients out and EVEN HAVE THE NERVE to sit down and write this book.

SO IF YOU FEEL DISCOURAGED LET THIS HELP YOU OUT, I WALK AND HAVE WALKED IN YOUR SHOES AND I HAVE MANY STORIES!

One of my success secrets is BEING TALKED ABOUT (MY FAVORITE) because I know I will end up doing something else that they cannot handle and they will question themselves, how is he doing that? NONE OF YOUR BUSINESS what they are really doing is giving me their life essence so attention is drawn in my direction and not theirs and this is why I love this kind of behavior, you should think about it this way. I'VE GAINED MANY CLIENTS BECAUSE OF THIS. SO DO NOT BE DISCOURAGED

These tools let me see things differently so they would be able to benefit my business as well as myself. I've also included biblical business references and they have actually worked as well for me if something would happen to go wrong.

You need to read a' lot of uplifting books, so you can get to the next level, surround yourself with peers who's visions, ideas and dreams sound as coo coo as yours trust me they are going in a forward direction as well and are walking alone, if they question your motives why are you doing that and begin with oh nobody is going to buy that etc. GET RID OF THEM, FLUSH THE TOILET!

DO NOT REVEAL YOUR VISION OR SECRET only amongst the like thinkers!

Trust me I know many have questioned me especially when I started selling high end hair they would say no one is really going to buy that or can afford it to try and discourage me .. My answer: NO YOU WILL NOT BUY IT AND CAN'T AFFORD IT also THEY WILL AUTOMATICALLY TELL ON THEMSELVES letting you know how they feel about you with these remarks, big difference and the clientele I'm specifically targeting are not walking in your shoes... OH DID YOUR JAW JUST DROP then I was talking about you.

If you cater to a specific clientele and start targeting and looking for them, they will find you remember they are looking for quality not what's the cheapest and quickest.

You will find yourself alone many times, many will not understand your walk however that's ok, this walk is for you, so you're able to stand out and they will not be able to stand in your light.

I am always questioning myself, HOW DO I GET TO THAT STEP? Even with the budget being extremely tight.

1. I BELIEVE IT, so it's going to happen
2. THE FINANCES will be there even when it looks like it's not, your heart has to be in the right place.

3. Be able to HELP someone out a COMPLETE STRANGER without no one knowing that you had performed the deed, nor are you to speak about it, remember your day of need is coming so begin opening this door.
4. LEARN to have an INQUISITIVE MIND and QUESTION EVERYTHING that seems complicated and makes no sense. The answer usually is right in front of you.
5. DO NOT WALK WITH ANYONE WHOS NOT WALKING IN YOUR DIRECTION!

And if you decide for someone to join in make sure they are also going in a forward direction, if this person includes themselves in your journey to encourage you make out the habits they have and what their agenda is, more than likely they will tell on themselves. You do not have to be doing the same thing to be together but actually

Moving in a forward direction if it's a struggle and it's fighting you it's not meant for you. NEITHER ARE FOLLOWERS.

FIND YOUR NICHE' and PERFECT IT, I am proof that I have found mine even though I cater too many. I JUST WROTE IT OUT FOR YOU.

This walk is not for A CO'DEPENDANT PERSON or the like it will be ALONE for the most part!

YOU ARE FEARFULLY AND WONDERFULLY CREATED *PSALM 139: 14*, as it is written that's why there's no need for CO'DEPENDANCY or to be INCLUDED .....

And remember GOD CAN ONLY GIVE YOU AS FAR AS YOUR EYES CAN SEE ......GENESIS 13:14

HI SCOTTY

This is one of those things that I typically keep to myself, do not care to share with others or admit to. It brings me personal joy and it's MY SECRET.

In the prior chapter I stated to try and help someone out, reason being you will never know where your help or in which direction your help will be coming from or when your day of need will be!

Ivy (not her name) happens to be a homeless woman that walks around Montclair, NJ; I've known about her since the 90's, it amazes me how people just walk by her as if she's nonexistent.

I'm not sure about her story and what happened to her; she actually brings a balance to me and just happens to put things in perspective. I've seen her in rags during the summer and throughout the year roaming aimlessly at times, or just sitting on a bench just looking out. Each and every time I do encounter her, I try and spend 5 minutes of my time with her, just to give her some sort of attention so she is aware some stranger at least cares and acknowledges her existence. DO NOT BE FOOLED THIS CAN BE YOU.

I also give her some money so she's able to get something to eat and drink she really doesn't know who I am and lovingly calls me SCOTTY! As I stated you do not know where your help, healing or open door will be coming from. So it's best not to look down for in turn you'll look foolish.

So here's how this works: HELPING IVY

1. Opens doors for me
2. Helps me sleep peacefully at night
3. Heals me
4. Secures me financially
5. Gives me FAVOR in someone else's eyesight

6. Allows many opportunities to say yes to me
7. Shows me how to forgive

And this list can go on. I will say this when opportunity presented itself to me I was available for it things had a way of working themselves out especially when it came time to acquiring my 3rd business. I truly do not like speaking about this secret, but it is essential for you to know how, it's possible for me to maintain my business be somewhat successful and be able to encourage the reader who is self employed and trying to figure it out, I work alone no outside help aside from my loyal clients that come from every walk of life.

No one ever wanted to work with me, or just be around me these things never did or ever will matter to me. It just truly showed me how ENVIOUS you are of me, and they weren't even occupying the outer peripheral of my conscious to acknowledge that behavior, this also goes for the ones that like to compare themselves to me when we're out, If you're reading this book out of curiosity we don't compare you wouldn't be able to catch up still stuck on trying to figure it out!

As long as someone like IVY exists and I STEP OUT IN FAITH, I HAVE A DIVINE CONNECTION and am able to move THE HAND OF GOD!

MORAL OF THE STORY:
The poor will be with you always. MARK 14:7
I have just revealed a BIBLICAL SECRET to you!
So remember your day is coming
SO DO NOT FORGET TO HELP IVY OUT!
This also will have to be done in a gracious manner expecting NOTHING and I mean NOTHING in return, you should be happy just doing it.

KEEP IT A SECRET ….. Or else it will all be in vain…………

THE TWO WOMEN RESPONSIBLE FOR THE VISION WITHIN THE BOOK!

One woman is and was living with cancer and has transitioned.

The other woman just happens to be a single mother with children making it work to the best of her ability.

I am only able to focus on these two women on my own, no one really understands or care too. You see in my mind these two women actually have become one woman.

So if it wasn't for my aunt going through her ordeal and my mother being a single parent. I would not have been able to focus on this specific woman and be able to help her out to the best of my ability.

And this is how the: VIDA DE MIRTE FOUNDATION will be born in translation THE LIFE OF MIRTE FOUNDATION, to aid and assist single mothers raising their children while living with cancer!

This is why it's essential to STAND OUT BY YOURSELF so you can be THE ATTENTION!

BECAUSE OF THEM I'M ABLE TO CONSULT AND CATER TO THESE WOMEN WITH TOTAL UNDERSTANDING AND NO JUDGEMENT.

BECAUSE OF YOU PURCHASING THIS BOOK THESE THINGS CAN HAPPEN AND ACTUALLY BRIGHTEN A WORLD THAT IS RATHER DARK AT TIMES…………………………………………..

COLLEEN GAREY TO THE
IRIE BEAUTY EXPO

As I mentioned earlier be careful how you treat somebody, because you never know where your help will be coming from as well as your favor.

A little over 10 years ago while I was still in my original location, I had received a phone call from Colleen who had come across my old website she recalls phonebook. I had answered told her she was speaking to me, from what I recall she stated I NEED YOUR HELP and I KNOW YOU CAN HELP ME! I was a little taken back; I really didn't know her nor what kind of help I would've been able to assist her with. She briefed me that she had a wig salon in Virginia but she had run into a problem trying to repair/alter a wig for a client. I said ok I'm in NJ you're in VA how is this going to happen?

It just so happened Colleen had reached out to me at a perfect time, I was signed up to take a wig altering course and of all places Washington D.C. she lived in VA!

In this business many stylist are cut throat about self nor do they care about sharing information with other stylist! I had nothing to lose and something about Colleen felt right to me so I told her it just so happens I'm taking this course why don't you meet me, it's in 2 weeks since its right in your backyard let's take it together.

We automatically clicked on the phone an instantly connected in person, we've been in contact ever since!

She is now CEO of IRIEEXTENSIONS HAIR ENTERPRISE has a successful hair wafting educational course and additional hair salon in Florida.

Fast forward she had reached out to me so I can be aware she's going to take a bigger challenge and create her own BEAUTY EXPO which is a HUGE UNDERTAKING.

She had asked me if I would be interested in lecturing, I said sure might as well strike while the iron is hot!

She put me on board with her celebrity line up, lil' ole me with my dream of consulting salons/stylists with their clients dealing with hair loss while living with cancer.

So in retrospect I could've been a total jackass, like many of these stylist who don't care in sharing information over 10 years ago took the wig altering class, never would've told her, met up with her in DC to train her,charge her for my time leaving her clueless about that.

That's the STYLIST JACKASS I could've been but COLLEENS spirit felt right to me and I didn't, I blessed her with the info and she in turn decided to have me stand before beauty world royalty to be one of them at her IRIE MEGA BEAUTY EXPO

Moral of the story:
Proverbs 22:29
Do you see a man skilled in his work?
He will stand in the presence of kings; he will not stand in the PRESENCE OF UNKNOWN MEN!

THANK YOU MA'CHERIE'
YOU WERE HEAVEN SENT
COLLEEN GAREY CAN BE FOUND AT:

WEFTING HAIR TRAINING
137 BELLAGIO CIRCLE
SANFORD, FLORIDA
1-407-878-2162
WWW.HAIRWEFTINGTRAINING.COM
WWW.IRIEXTENSION.COM

Colleen Garey Irie hair expo on panel

THE INTERNATIONAL ASSOCIATION OF TRICHOLOGY

Conference

The day had come 6/27 /16; I have lived to speak at this conference. To begin with the conference was being held at the legendary DRAKE HOTEL in CHICAGO. Opulence is an understatement I arrived on the Saturday; though my flight was delayed I had enough time to rehearse my lecture at the airport for the millionth time!

This was to be a 2 day conference. I had checked in settled in my room and decided to walk around the property as well as lake shore drive, my mind was racing in disbelief that this day has arrived even though I have a charismatic,animated personality that's more happy go lucky.

I've spoken in front of groups before, but now I kept thinking everything will change for me. For starters it didn't hit me till that day, I was on a panel of distinguished PROFESSIONAL DR'S from around the world, think about it GLOBAL, I'm sure a few were trying to figure out who I was, however it didn't matter what mattered was they were interested in what I had to say!

For most of that Saturday I was exhausted from travel, but throughout the cab ride to the airport, waiting for the flight, on the plane, arriving getting out of the airport, heading to the hotel, checking in, going out walking around my emotions were getting the best of me.

As I walked down lake shore drive and headed to get something to eat at PORTILLO'S all I kept thinking about was that Saturday afternoon I got home from work and my aunt was in the kitchen chatting away with my mom. I kept hearing her laughter and she teasing me about getting a mule since I didn't have a car, asking her to take a picture with me sitting on her lap, so I can eternally have it!

Alone with her asking me the ultimate question CAN YOU HELP ME WITH MY HAIR?

I could not believe it I have gone from sitting on her lap, not being able to answer her question to presenting alongside dignified professionals in their fields of hair loss at a GLOBAL HAIR LOSS CONFERENCE, to presenting in front of a room of people ANSWERING HER QUESTION?

I could not stop tearing up for 2 whole days just thinking about this. The next day I was happy to see many of my colleagues and friends that I knew from all over and many were excited to hear what I had to say. When I had entered that grand conference room I really had become overwhelmed, especially since the room was incredibly ornate, gold gilded columns, chandeliers, etc and the room looked as if it could go on forever, I mean way over the top for a conference. But I relished in it.

It actually was the vision I kept having since my AUNT had asked that question as well as how FABULOUS FERNANDO and I were going to become.

To the reader this might sound silly but to me it was a reality. It had actually COME TO LIFE! It felt rather weird that Andrea wasn't there.

Monday 6/27 /16 all the lectures were great and I had my favorites, I was to be 2nd to closing the conference. That Monday morning David (IATpres.) and his wife Sue had asked me when my book will be complete; I answered the minute I get off that stage.

I was given only 45 minutes to lecture and to be able to answer questions, it was time for me to go up I stood in front of everyone and dove right into my lecture, I surprisingly was not nervous considering how overwhelmingly ornate and grand the room was!

I had to accept it since I kept envisioning GRAND well the ALL FATHER gave me GRAND, right there JEHOVAH JIRAH said well isn't this what you wanted?

I gave my lecture answered the questions, I thought about how I didn't introduce myself and basically said a quiet thank you, I had asked David to turn around and look at the last slide. The lecture was dedicated to my late aunt's memory, it was also to thank Sue and himself for making a 20 yr. old kid sitting on his aunts lap very happy and for all to see it!

I really did not recall anyone clapping nor saying anything it was as if I was silenced. I got off the stage walked into the other room to use the bathroom get it together and came back and sat down to listen to David finish lecturing and give his closing remarks.

I noticed many were smiling at me. But I really had no idea the impact that I had when everything was over, many members came and flocked to hug me one particularly a blonde immediately sat next to me holding back her tears and thanking me for addressing the issue she had told me, she had lost her mother to breast cancer and though she was a stylist didn't understand how to help her, another member a man I didn't even know grabbed to compliment me and started to cry about how this touched him hugging me, the DR'S that were on the panel were so happy they just kept hugging, kissing and complimenting me.

But interestingly the ones I least expected anything from kept hugging me continuously thanking me, it was surreal.

The next morning I decided to get up early and walk down to the lakefront to gather my thoughts the task had been completed, It had come and gone so quickly just like that however it wasn't finished yet I had further to go since it was beginning . I had been invited to lecture in other countries around the U.S. and Caribbean Islands.

I had happen to run into David and Sue at the post office in the Sears Towers I had said good morning wished them well on their journey back home to Australia . David had a smile on his face Sue as well and had thanked me for doing such an excellent job and how the lecture was well received.

That's all I needed, upon returning to the hotel 1 member that I see every year a stoic ultra conservative man we hardly speak to one another outside of a hello, was sitting in a chair had fixed his gaze on me I said good morning to him he had a huge smile shook my hand and said he enjoyed my lecture WELL DONE!

I WAS ELATED!

I HAD DREAMED A DREAM AND IT CAME TRUE!

Lecturing at the Drake Hotel in Chicago

THE MOTHS

7/4/16, this time the week prior I had accomplished the vision that I had desired to complete and it had come to pass!

I decided that the best place to finish writing my book and give my closing remarks was at my cousin Betsy's beautiful home in the mountains near the Catskills, a perfect place to gather my thoughts, I love how her wrap around deck looks out over a hill down to a creek an all that I can see beyond the creek.

The journey has not been easy writing this book made me realize how much I had inside me that needed to be birthed. What a difference a year makes, this time the prior year I was with my best friend MANNY of nearly 30 years who I just adore celebrating the 4th at rainbow mountain in the Poconos even though I might had looked happy, had a good time there, I was actually melancholy, upset over every ordeal that I had gone through the year prior as well as considering not to go to the IAT CONFERENCE, since then I had moved my business the November before a feat that any business owner can relate to truly understand and getting adjusted .

That November of 2015 I had been asked to be interviewed for the DWILDMUSICRADIO show, April 2015 I was filmed for the documentary MY HAIR MY VOICE, the new year especially the first 4 months were turbulent rollercoaster financially as if something was still holding me back not to speak at the conference. During that year I associated myself with STATEWIDE HISPANIC CHAMBER OF COMMERCE was awarded a 12 week business program that I had completed before heading to conference, I also was awarded a 9 month business course through RUTGERS UNIVERSITY I have another 5 months to go as I'm writing this book . I am truly being aligned for the birthing process that will happen.

On 7/13/15 was my graduation through the chamber I decided to remain as humble an quiet about who OZZY really is, however the week prior I decided to present in front of the entire class to encourage them to hold on to their VISION, DREAM be LATIN & PROUD you are actually looking at a miracle who is not only a national speaker but an international one as well, my class couldn't believe it and were cheering me on.

Look at all the things that happened through my personal pain. This book took longer than I had anticipated since I kept receiving more chapters to add to it. I also wanted to walk down from that stage at THE DRAKE HOTEL in CHICAGO in all its OPULENCE! I was saddened that the year that Andrea should've been there she was not able it was so surreal, since we had made the pact to keep moving forward!

My lecture belonged to me through the promise that I had been keeping in my spirit for over 20yrs for my aunt, cousin Betsy's mom this is why it was important for me to stay at your house July 4th weekend.

It was a perfect setting peaceful quiet especially MOTH HAPPY. We had a great day went to brunch at the BEAR MOUNTAIN INN you decided we should sit out on the balcony to eat THE MOTHS started coming you started swatting them, let's go take a walk around the lake, WHY ARE ALL THESE MOTHS AROUND ? I've never see so many of them and they're attracted to me!

The moths kept escalating, even as we went back to the house, how interesting that a number of them kept being attracted to your office window right where TIA'S /MY AUNT /YOUR MOM'S graduation picture hangs on the side wall, actually they were a sign .

Moths are symbolic much like a butterfly but not as pretty the reason there were so many is they were happy we were together, the reason they were surrounding us this was TIA'S your MOMMY'S SMILE coming through the escalation to prove to you the effect how many women I will impact through my product line as well as this book. I conquered one goal here's the other.

I wasn't given an international platform for no reason!

All will hear the call and all will come to aid and help many!

TIA WAS HAPPY..... She was aware

THAT I KEPT MY PROMISE!

SOME MORE THANK YOUS

DR. ROSE ANN DIOS
Associate Professor
Mathematical sciences
NJIT

I would like to personally thank you through this book. I haven't see you in years, however through writing this book I started recalling the time when Ronny and I helped you get your dissertation together in NY, it was actually my first time in the big city.

You were prepping your book to print so you could defend it for your PHD. I remember that like it was yesterday, If memory serves me right Ronnie and I were like 12 or 13, you had promised us that if we helped you get this together you were going take us to GREAT ADVENTURES (this is all we cared about).

THANK YOU for always being a BEAM OF LIGHT through my childhood, I will never forget that and I'm truly honored to have been part of your journey while writing my own book.

I hope I haven't disappointed.

LOVE AND GOD BLESS YOU

OZZY

OLU FAJEMIROKUN BECK
CEO. BECKPROPERTIES INC.
WHOLESOME SWEETENERS
WWW.WHOLESOMESWEET.COM
NETWORK OF EXECUTIVE WOMEN

Thank you for always being a source of INSPIRATION!

Always encouraging me even if my ideas come off as crazy, especially with the T.M.I moments which you are well aware are my favorites.

Even giving an ear to my views on worldly events and investigative reporting's.

Not one to pass judgments.

There are 3 words that you always and continuously express to me; they forever ring in my ears.

I truly love you for this push, so because of you

I can: GO FOR IT and I did!

GOD BLESS YOU

LOVE

OZZY

LUCIA CEZIMBRA

The sister I never had but always has been, we have been inseparable since high school always rolling your eyes at me, tuning me out with my all my nonstop talking. Well guess what I'M STILL TALKING!

I LOVE YOU for always being there for me, anyone who can go to a 1 a.m. showing of LORD OF THE RINGS: return of the king 3.5hr movie and put up with that dreadful STONE ROCK ISLAND trip and not say a word except I'M DOG TIRED will always remain next to me.

We're oil and water, frick & frack, loud & silent.

We can practically be together all day not say a word to each other and have the best time together, knowing that works my last nerve.

But I wouldn't change nothing I LOVE IT AND I LOVE YOU

GOD BLESS YOU

OZZY

P.S. tell slumlord to please fix that bottom doorknob on the front door k.

LESLIE SHORT
K.I.M MEDIA LLC&DESIGN BY KIM
www.kim-media.com
www.leslieshort.com

To a TRUE ORIGINAL ...THANK YOU, THANK YOU, THANK YOU!

You've been encouraging me since the early 90's (am I telling our age, lol), to step up my game, always there to give me your true honest criticism and never judging me!

Many in your position would be self centered and could have cared less but not you, always lending your ear to give me positive direction.

You are a true genuine person and I'm grateful for as well as value our friendship

GOD BLESS YOU
LOVE YOU LOTS, LOTS
OZZY
WWW.TARGETMARKETINGMAG.COM/POST/
FIRSTMARKETERDAYMONDJOHNEVERHIRED

TANYA FREEMAN ESQ.

PARTNER OF WEINER LESNIAK LLP
629 PARSIPPANY ROAD
PARSIPPANY, NJ 07054
1-201-228-9867
WWW.TANYAFREEMANESQ.COM

As time progressed I always wanted to publicly acknowledge you and at the same time keep you a secret, then the time came, to write a review on a legal site and I still felt it wasn't the right time. Then you were selected as ATTNY OF THE YEAR! And as life would have it seasons come and go.

People are always looking at the book cover and never bother to look at the pages within the book; I can truly say I've witnessed the pages within the book and within these pages you will be acknowledged. I've witnessed you carrying all your depositions into my studio, working diligently, handling the phone calls whether with your clients and or your 6 children, going to school, volunteering your time etc. we've been together at 6 am and at midnight STILL WORKING and for the most part Nonstop.

It always amazed me and at the same time discretely taking your advice with nothing being said, just paying attention to everything you were doing.

Always encouraging me that we have to move forward, what's the next step? We have to keep climbing, become an octopus keep involved in as much as you can business wise, etc.

I wanted to wait till this book came out; I found myself 23hrs away on the other side of the planet in New Zealand and if my Brand was known there I wanted your Brand known there as well for each and every person holding this book because we all know there's always more room to grow your brand

One thing I encounter from time to time is women letting me in on how their husbands accuse them for getting cancer not supporting them through this time, finding any excuses to keep up appearances because this is not what they signed up for . OH YES THEY DID, its part of the COMPROMISE in marriage. Well here is your GO TO DIVORCE ATTNY for anyone dealing with this B.S. ....

MR.FREEMAN is a FORTUNATE MAN to have a wife like you; he actually has a SECRET TREASURE......

My REVIEW or THANK YOU couldn't be any greater

THANK YOU for always being there for me, never judging me even when things became a bit chaotic....being supportive is an understatement

GOD BLESS YOU
LOVE
OZZY

YOUTUBE: TANYA FREEMAN WEINER LESNIAK

TRAVELING TO PUERTO RICO

As I mentioned earlier I had made my peace with my father, so thanksgiving week of 2015 went very well. I had the best time visiting my family, spending time with my mom as well as my brothers.

But spending time with my father seemed interesting to me he wasn't sure how to react to me, I was physically in his presence, being my typical self (LONER) which in turns means I do not care to be bothered.

So remember what I had said in a prior chapter about regret. I actually pitied him for wasting valuable time and had to stand in my presence full of regret. He had spoken to me again apologizing and had also wanted to apologize to my mother as well, so I just looked at him and kindly told him.

You will need to live with the decisions you have made throughout your entire life, something's are just best left alone!

I realized I want to be better than that so when I transition from this earth, I have left my mark and have kept my integrity.

MORAL OF THE STORY:

Make sure you are able to eat from the same dish you have served, for it will surprise you and return with a complete tea service.

NEW ZEALAND

Wow, well I made the commitment, which was fighting me for a complete year, not sure if I was going through with this.

And since the stars aligned it was possible again the doors were opened, the airfare became reasonable even with an upgrade and where I stayed which only happened to be a block away from the conference. Not in a million years did I even expect to be on the other side of the planet 23 hrs away.

As I'm writing this I'm still in disbelief that I actually went through with it.

The day came that I spoke at the conference, the night before I had added extra slides to my presentation, Diana (finddiana.com) came with me as well and had witnessed my lecture. I was happy to see other familiar faces there.

I made a commitment and fulfilled it: I KEPT MY PROMISE!

David & Sue (IATdirectors) trusted me with this, yes they took a chance and a risk not knowing what the outcome was going to be back in Chicago, however it was a success so here I was in the present time .

To add to this there were some that really do not nor do I care understand my walk, I say this because a few were trying to discourage me from even speaking in Chicago saying subliminal negative comments about the conference.

Thankfully I for one am adamant, strong willed and usually follow my tenacious instinct.

As I said I'm following my spiritual direction, these plans were already laid out so here's a bit of advice to the naysayers!

It's up to you to figure out how to take advantage and utilize what has been offered to you! I WAS KEEPING A PROMISE

Please do not limit your vision and see the bigger picture for yourself.

Since then I have been offered many opportunities, been acknowledged by Dr's from around the world within the IAT and outside as well.

These things can also happen to you if you avoid being a crab in a barrel and begin removing yourself from yourself, YOU GET IN YOUR OWN WAY!

I always knew I was going to speak in front of many people about this topic that is rather difficult to grasp and understand. I just didn't know which door was going to be opened for me but I held on to my faith, so here's where I can only say that I have DEEP GRATITUDE am HUMBLE as well as GRATEFUL towards DAVID & SUE while all others where ridiculing me, not sure of me , didn't take me serious they saw beyond that .

THAT LUNCH DATE AT THE HILLWOOD ESTATE AND CHICAGO GAVE BIRTH TO THIS BOOK IN TURN CHANGED MY LIFE!

Log in to the info below if you ever want to further your studies in understanding hair loss.

International Association of Trichologist
185 Elizabeth St
Sydney, NSW 2000
+61 2 9267 1384
http://www.trichology.edu.au/

You can purchase all these items at the above address

HAIR LOSS HANDBOOK 2014
HAIRDRESSING SCIENCE LECTURES

THE HAIR AND SCALP 2012 (Illustrated with diagrams and photos)

HAIR LOSS & SCALP PROBLEMS (USB of 43 photos

I'm also featured in HAIRY TALES:
Trichologists from around the world tell their stories

David Salinger and Sue Erickson

Lecturing at the crown plaza in auckland, nz

NEVER BE DISCOURAGED

If I was able to have an impact and impress a Dr. all the way in MUMBAI, INDIA ....SO CAN YOU ....BELIEVE IN YOUR GIFT . That's why GOD GAVE IT TO YOU!

I first met Ozzy at the International Trichology meeting in Chicago. It is impossible to overlook his towering personality, but the moment you interact, you immediately appreciate his gentle demeanor. His presentation was thorough in understanding of his clients. He has made special effort to understand the different types of cancer treatments the clients would be going through. He has gained skills in understanding the grief and the changing thoughts of the clients. He has a detail analysis and planned approach to make the clients comfortable, feeling at home with him during the consultation with professional as well as emotional interaction. Ozzy has a knack of finding useful information and providing it to serve the need of his clients plus the community. Every time I meet him he has made some more additions to his skills and knowledge. I wish him all the best and pray that he continues to have this insatiable appetite for finding new useful information to share with all of us.

Regards, Dr Rajesh Rajput, Rajendrasingh, MS, MCh, Plastic Surgeon, Hair Transplant Surgeon, Fellow ISHRS - USA, Trichologist IAT, Pioneer Cyclical Vitamin Therapy for Hair Regrowth (Hair Fact Kits) Hair Restore Clinic, Bandra, Mumbai, (India) www.hairlossindia. com, drrajeshrarjput@gmail.com

HOW LONG WILL THIS BE FOR?

Make sure you are ready for the answer if you have just asked the question!

As I was interviewing the daughter who had lost her mother years prior this was 1 of 2 things that really stood out through the entire chat. So to make a long story short, this will be mainly be geared towards anyone who happens to think like this.

When the wife's mother had become terminally ill, her husband had become curious to know HOW LONG THE ILLNESS WILL LAST, HOW LONG WILL SHE BE IN OUR CARE? To me it sounded more of a matter of appearances than the reality. This for one is a psychological effect for the person not affected by it. They walk around as if life is grand and nothing is going to touch them and life is to remain perfect.

Not to specifically point him out for he's 1 in a 100 so he's not alone, I've heard worse on how it was the wife's fault she had cancer and they start having affairs outside the marriage to keep their perfect appearance, so this is mild.

This question kept arising, the wife was a mother of 2 small children and at the time the mother had come to live with them for a time. SO HOW LONG WILL THIS BE AND LAST FOR? I do not want the children to experience this nor know about it.

After a while the mother was moved to hospice which the daughter had been totally against and detested doing, for she wanted to care for her, shortly after months in hospice her mom had transitioned. The day of her transition the daughter had a gnawing feeling to be with her mother, her husband needed the car that morning she would need to wait for him to get back then she could go about her business to care for her mom. But as fate would have it exactly when the husband came back home the phone had rung, he had answered and the news was delivered directly to him!

He was granted the responsibility to deliver the news to his wife, her mother had transitioned.

You see he kept asking the question HOW LONG WILL THIS BE FOR? So he received the answer and was selected to deliver it!

MORAL OF THE STORY:

This was done as a lesson and to advise others

The flip side, through this trying time was how the mother / daughter relationship had blossomed, before any of this they had their disagreements and usually not always on the same page. But the mother had revealed a secret to her daughter that she kept hidden within and while the daughter continued taking care of her it was revealed. She told her, she never realized HOW BEAUTIFUL SHE REALLY WAS the validation had been AFFIRMED!

FINDING THE STRENGTH IN MYRA

Myra (not her real name) was young, beautiful, energetic and successful. The 90's so many opportunities so little time not one to make a private matter a public thing. Being an up & coming celebrity in the 90's you did not disclose your medical conditions or be at risk of being denied employment in the acting field!

I was fortunate enough to be granted this interview by her mother not knowing what to expect and how transparent she was going to be especially with being accepting that she was GOD'S CHILD, and mommy was only babysitting! Wow.

Time was the biggest role and Myra's greatest accomplishment during that time; she was adamant about receiving any toxic medication and did not want to live her life like that. Her mom was supportive as possible and joined her child with this fight and whatever the fight would be.

It was Myra's decision though others were advising her to take a different direction. Her decision was she wanted life as normal as possible and to be as encouraging as possible.

Myra encouraged others that they deserved a shot, to branch out go further at success a close friend felt she never had received her just do's of who she was, the talent and the beautiful person that she had become .

She was right in not telling them, she made the rules, wanted you to hear about life and the meaning of it. The fight to stand by your truth for you were there to listen to her, to be there through the challenges try to work it out with a friend knowing that you didn't care.

At the end Myra made the choice of what she wanted to do the beauty of it was she was not able to begin the treatment and the time had run out.

She lived the life that she wanted towards the end and said ok let's do the chemo even though she wasn't well enough. She was in control of everything had waited to the very end and it took over decided to do it now, since she chose to not go through traditional medicine to save herself.

Is this the answer you were looking for you are here to listen to me and once she was beyond the illness there was a reflection period one day you will face the same destiny.

So while life is still present LIVE IT WITH LOVE, LIVE IT WITHOUT FEAR AND LIVE YOUR TRUTH.......................

LOVE MYRA.........................

FINDING HOPE WHEN IT SEEMS THERE IS NONE!

I for one have an inquisitive mind and love to do extensive research just to get answers, in any case you can lead a horse to water but you cannot make them drink.

Before you go further this chapter is based on HOPE, not saying that this is a CURE however these are proven facts.

Here are some of many of my go to resources and hopefully they will help you in your journey as well at the end of the day it is best to have your clients or family members health best interest at heart.

BOOKS TO READ:

1. CANCER IT'S CAUSE AND CURE – DR.OTTO WARBURG
2. THE GERSON THERAPY: DR.MAX GERSON
3. A CANCER THERAPY: results of 50 cases and the cure for advanced cancer DR. MAX GERSON

Even though there are many books to read on how to live holistically healthy lifestyle while living with cancer. These are my top 3 books furthermore they have been around since the late 40's while studying Trichology, I found understanding MITOSIS-CELL DIVISION very interesting to me I came across how cancer was first identified in WNT SIGNALING : which is the dual function protein that communicate with each other when the hair follicle is being formed this lead me to how Dr. Warburg figured out that SUGAR was creating a perfect environment for cancer to live in while Dr. Gerson through his natural diet explained how regular SALT was causing the cells to multiply at a rapid rate . And in further studying this how I came across Dr. Bernardo Majalca and THE IMPORTANCE OF AN ALKALINE DIET which in turn just made total sense when you understand the PH SCALE that is second nature when chemically treating hair and bringing back to the natural ph balance through NEUTRALIZING, simple math being knowledgeable in ACIDITY and ALKALINITY and this is how I connected the dots.

Always test PH BALANCE from your saliva to check for acidosis the body's ph balance is the KEY TO HEALTH.

You should also read:
WORLD WITHOUT CANCER: The story of VITAMIN B17 by EDWARD GRIFFIN I and II

BOOKS IN PDF:

1. THOUSAND PLANTS AGAINST CANCER : GUISEPPI NACCI M.D. –MEDICAL BASED EVIDENCE
2. DR. BERNARDO MAJALCA PDF : free copy of Dr.Majalca's healing plan
3. THE NITRILOSIDES (VITAMIN B-17): ERNST KREBS JR

LECTURES TO WATCH ON YOU TUBE:
CHARLOTTE GERSON: Dramatic news from Charlotte Gerson
Healing with amazing results
Healing Supposedly incurable diseases

DANNY VIERA: True art of healing
God's health plan 1 through 3

THE INCURABLE WEBISODE: a girl, cancer & the doctor who knew how to heal her.
BRIAN SCOTT PESKINS: The hidden story of cancer
This book can also be purchased under the same title.

INSPIRATIONAL DOCUMENTARIES TO BUY OR WATCH
THESE YOU CAN WATCH FOR FREE ON YOU TUBE:
1.   THE GERSON MIRALCE
2.   WHAT IS MORE TERRIFYING THAN CANCER-THE
     CURE
BARBARA O'NEIL: author, educator, qualified naturopath and
nutritionist, is also an international speaker on natural self-healing. http://
www.barbhealth.com/, https://www.mmh.com.au

Has great lectures on cleansing and eating healthy.

MY PEOPLE ARE DESTROYED FROM THEIR LACK OF
KNOWLEDGE! HOSEA 4:6

Please consult with your medical professional with the following
references and chapters. Many Dr's now are including Integrative Medical
Therapies to assist with your well being, so it doesn't hurt to ask.

I'M BEING TALKED ABOUT

But no one is listening, I thought I was finished writing this book 6/12/17 but as I reflect, you really don't know what I encounter when consulting a client starting or going through chemo and need guidance on selection of hair .

As I sit to consult with them their eyes start welling up as if they begin crying but suddenly they catch themselves and stop right there as if a wall went up. Being highly intuitive and empathic their silence actually speaks to me, just the tears and me this is why I forbid stylist not to begin with the crying! What her silence is telling me she thinks it's the end, NEVER!

The other factor is I consistently think about my aunt and reflect on how she looked at me, if I had all this knowledge then imagine how much longer she could've been with us.

BELIEF, HOPE AND FAITH is a HUGE POWER and if exercised correctly can do severe damage to your opponent! This is why I KEPT MY PROMISE, BECAUSE OF YOU TIA MIRTE'

Since I don't have a love life, I don't ever see myself getting married *quoting* WHY COMPROMISE, WHAT IS THAT? (EARTHA KITT) nor have children, my nieces and nephews are more than enough for me as well as all the little kids that pay me a visit to see MR. OZZY.

I engrossed myself in research and was led to write, one thing I usually do when I get up every day is THANK GOD/JESUS for another day and to PROTECT MY HEALTH the 2nd request is for KNOWLEDGE and WISDOM everything else follows.

Not realizing that it would explode into extensive research of reading, listening to lectures and a majority of them are very boring especially from a DR'S point of view, but I am guided to LISTEN.

You'll be surprised what you'll discover in just reading, research and listening to SNOOZEFEST boring lectures

I seek out *TRACE EVIDENCE* and before you know it a DR. will relate something technical that speaks directly to me and I found what I was looking for and to think this all stemmed from behind the chair designing styling wigs, studying trichology, hair loss, cell division and WNT SIGNALING (explained in a earlier chapter)

So what triggered this new chapter? 1ˢᵗ I came across a book called THE IMMORTAL LIFE OF HENRIETTA LACKS also known as HELA CELLS written by REBECCA SKLOOT. I found this story fascinating and dove right in even to the point I found a old gritty documentary from the early 70's about her done by DR'S on this subject and to say the least very and I mean very boring unless you know what you're looking for. I watched it several times just to find what I was looking for and as fate would have it WA'LA 1 of the Dr's spoke directly to me to give me an answer

Many and I do mean many wondrous things were done with her cells; they are the only cells in existence that can be experimented on outside of the human body this is where cultured cells/cells tested in petri'dishes stem from. You can even buy them online billions of her cells are still in existence. But the beauty of her cells that really caught my attention is that they multiply at a RAPID RATE (I break this down in my lecture)

How to cater to a woman who is losing her hair while living w/cancer

What I found interesting was the timeline of this person when they were experimenting with her and her cells, since this was the late 40's early 50's the other thing in the boring documentary the relationship between the Russian and American Dr's another clue, explaining the breakthroughs and their relationship.

So there was #1 of asking for knowledge and wisdom ask and it shall be given to you knock and the door shall be opened MATHEW 7:7-8.

#2 I started coming across articles of Dr's, Naturopaths Holistic and Homeopathic Dr's either dying mysteriously, killed or missing.

So what on God's green earth is going on? I found this very disturbing but of course I focused to find some answers for myself. Thankfully after reading THE MAX GERSON THERAPY watching THE GERSON MIRACLE studying the PEPPER/NEELY ANTI-CANCER BILL 1875 from 1946 and THE CANCER LETTER of 1976 I understand why!

I always advise my clients to seek out a naturopath or holistic Dr. to work alongside their oncologist.

IT IS ILLEGAL IN THE U.S. to take on a patient that is under a Dr's care, however it is imperative to seek out someone that has the knowledge to build up your immune system! And introduce you to foods that are ELECTRIC..

For example I had a client coming to purchase a hair system who had open heart surgery many months prior asking the Dr. what she shall do with her hair that is falling out shedding excessively. She told me he brushed her away.

You do not ask for advice on HAIR with someone that is not knowledgeable about an area that is no thicker than a sheet of paper has 5 layers of skin, 1 capillary and 3 sweat glands for each strand of hair in an area that so microscopic and is only focusing on creating hair! This Dr's language was her chest within a 15 to 20 inch area THAT'S IT!

So the same applies to your Dr. they might be kind or not or just give you no answer. I pray that there would be some co or channel partnering with naturopaths / holistic Dr's.

I truly believe that if I want my DR to be a SUCCESS, I have to be the SUCCESS and this is only perfected when you're home.

Many doctors were making leaps and bounds treating cancer and a majority of them were actually doing well with great results. Many have passed on, so I decided to read, study and understand their theory.

In the U.S. if a DR. refuses to be labeled as a QUACK he must practice CONSENSUS MEDICINE meaning he must use the SAME MEDICINE used by his colleagues* CONSENSUS MEDICINE MUST BE USED BY EVERY PHYSYICIAN.

If a DR. deviates from this pattern to apply NUTRITION even if they have HIGH RATE SUCCESS he is CONDEMNED as a QUACK may lose hospital privileges even subject to arrest must *FOLLOW PROTOCOL* courtesy of: WORLD WITHOUT CANCER
*E.GRIFFIN 1974

So in response to pointing out the above quote printed in 1974, some things have changed you can download an entire PDF BOOK at:
https://www.cancer.gov/publications/patient-education/chemotherapy-and-you.pdf

this is for free from THE NATIONAL CANCER INSTITUTE PATIENT EDUCATION

You can also look up: NUTRITION IN CANCER CARE PDQ (patientversion)

https://www.cancer.gov/grants-training/training/funding:

they even offer training programs with grants that should be taken advantage of if interested in understanding this tricky world.

Two Dr's that caught my interest and came across while studying Vitamin D deficiencies, where Dr. John J. Bradstreet and Dr. Russel Blaylock their specialty Autism. I decided to read on Dr. Blaylock's reports on ENCEPHYLICTIC SCREAM and CYTAKIND STORM, cytakind really stood out to me so I kept reading on it.
You can find his report at *vaccinetruth.org*

CYTAKIND STORM: hits the body because it can't use VITAMIN D anymore causes brain to swell.

It caught my interest so here we go again it's all public information you just need to know what you're looking for willing to sit and listen to SNOOZEFEST lectures and Dr's and have a passion for reading so I will list all my references that I have become an admirer of.

I have come across much information trying to understand my clients and studying LAB SHEETS for VITAMIN DEFICIENCIES for TRICHOLOGY.

I am able to conduct my consultations more efficiently and have better understanding with what my client is going through.

What has been included in The Following chapters can be looked up and should be used for EDUCATIONAL PURPOSES the site is extensive but worth the time to read and get a better understanding.

EARLY DETECTION IS YOUR BEST DEFENSE!

In truth early detection, being knowledgeable about what is going on in your body is your best defense against any disease!

This is why it is imperative to know your BLOOD TYPE get YEARLY checkups and learn   to eat properly for your blood type

Anyone living with cancer, and going through need to understand that it takes almost 2 years for that treatment to be free from your body once treatment is completed.

Many have told me the reason they don't like to eat have loss of appetite is because what they are tasting a majority of the time is heavy metals.

This is why it is imperative to understand maintaining a healthy liver and learn how to detox and cleanse

Many are living with 2 conditions at 1 time, some cannot even incorporate an ALKALINE DIET into their regimen because of a specific autoimmune disorders.

So it's best to consult with your physician.

So let's back track why sugar must be omitted!

It CREATES a PERFECT ENVIORMENT for CANCER to THRIVE IN:

*removes all the oxygen from the blood stream

* creates HIGH ACIDITY and ACIDOSIS

CANCER CELLS do not commence and live by:
HYPOXIA – creates absence of the oxygen in the blood.

In order for it to survive/ keep producing ENEMY CELLS must switch over to:
GLYCOLYSIS- present in nearly all living organisms, GLUCOSE is the source of almost all energy used by cells.
GLUCOSE- is a simple sugar that is an important energy source in living organisms and is a component of many CARBOHYDRATES.

When FERMENTATION begins SICKENED distinctive cells must start protecting themselves from the IMMUNE SYSTEM!

THE MORE CANCER CELLS THE HIGHER FERMENATION PROCESS

The way to cut production of this enzyme is by the use of:

WINNING THE WAR AGAINST CANCER BEGINS WITH PERSONAL CHOICES!

- Reduce exposure to Pesticide, household chemical cleaners, synthetic air fresheners & air pollution
- Processed and artificial foods (plus the chemicals in the packaging)
- Wireless technologies, dirty electricity, and radiation exposure
- Obesity, stress, and poor sleeping habits
- Lack of sunshine exposure and use of sunscreens
- Eat cruciferous vegetables potent anti-cancer properties
- Maintain an ideal body weight
- Get high quality sleep
- Boil, poach or steam your foods, rather than FRYING or CHARBROILING them

Courtesy of: **Many Doctors Ignore the Root Cause of Cancer**
Author: *Dr. Joseph Mercola*
Publish date: Apr 6, 2009

If you're seeking advice when not sure here's a great go to source
Ralph Moss **on** Cancer--**Expert Guidance for Crucial Decisions**
www.ralphmoss.com/html/articles.shtml

he is the author of: CUSTOMIZED CANCER TREATMENT

this book alone is a WEALTH of information ,you can also visit:

http://cancerdecisions.com

GOD BLESS THIS MAN, I'M A FAN.INCREDIBLE actually every
DR'S name that I referenced here is a HERO.

There's a boatload of wonderful information out there so you don't feel
LOST, CONFUSED, ALONE or HOPELESS. This is why my favorites
are all added here so it's not overwhelming. I encounter so many clients
that go through those emotions that I've listed it can be a bit overwhelming
at times however I'm intellectually and emotionally strong enough to
handle it. So BE STRONG GRAB THE BULL BY THE HORNS
and WIN.............

These BRILLIANT DR'S DO EXIST!

I promised my AUNT I was going to find every imaginable answer
to her questions she was asking herself when no one was around at home
and she was alone in her room. Especially when she had to face her biggest
challenge when her Dr. had told her *THERES NOTHING ELSE WE
CAN DO*

Since 2002 I have been hunting and digging for all this information
that wasn't readily available in the early 90's as it is today!

YOU FOOLED ME

Is what GLYCONE sugar based complex molecule is.

We know that cancer cells LOVE SUGAR, so when the SALICINIUM passes by the cancer it GOBBLES IT UP.

SALICINIUM: does not kill or cure fermenting cells only the IMMUNE system can do that

Through the use of SALICINIUM can the immune system be returned to a FUNCTIONAL STATE!

This is also used as a IV NUTRITIONAL THERAPY, which is great because it goes directly into your blood stream and can absorb all the vital nutrients, much like the MAX GERSON THERAPY where he explains why it's important to get the correct juicer that separates the pulp from the liquid so upon drinking it, it goes directly into your blood stream This is very important because many women have loss of appetite and do not feel like eating however the nutrients need to be absorbed quickly!

Interestingly they also advise you to avoid taking high-doses Vitamin C supplements at the same time, whether by injection, IV, or orally.

Remember what was read in the previous chapters that when your body craves sugar it really wants VITAMIN C. read the instructions first.

As well as orally, you can look all the instructions at NATURODOC.BIZ

The use of Salicinium concurrently with conventional oncology is a matter requiring the judgment of a licensed and trained oncologist.

You can view the lecture on PRESENTING SALICINIUM – HOW IT WORKS on YOU TUBE
Courtesy of: https://www.salicinium.com/home.html

You can also read an article by:
CAROL M. BROWN
DO, PHD, FAARFM
Entitled – Salicinium / Excellent Addition to my
Armamentarium for Cancer Patients!

Armamentarium means:
The medicines, equipment, and techniques available to a medical practitioner

That was sure a whole lot of talk on SUGAR, now you see why it's so important to cut out all those CHEESECAKES, PASTRIES, COOKIES, TARTS all that delicious goodness.

You can view many lectures on Integrative Therapies at:

THETRUTH ABOUTCANCER
A Global Quest
By: TY M. BOLINGER
WWW.THETRUTHABOUTCANCER.COM

I had no clue I was going to come across so much information studying and researching for TRICHOLOGY. I set out to just write my story on basic advise and nutrition I DO NOT SLEEP the information just keeps coming to me even though through my research I came across a number of Dr's being accused of being quacks for making strides, there are many honest Dr's out there that do want the best for you! I decided let me be the judge I know how to read and seriously intrigued why   there's never a cure. With all that growth in the pharmaceutical world you have so many people suffering not knowing how they are going to pay their bills, keep a roof over their heads children life problems and living with illnesses. I was always curious to discover the secret of DANIELS DIET when I read it over and over it wasn't about losing weight it was about rebuilding your health and maintaining your youth.

I can truthfully say upon ending this chapter I HAVE KEPT MY PROMISE .... And it has become my SACRED DUTY to protect these women that are struggling financially raising their children alone that feel there's no hope, with knowledge, wisdom and discover as much information, help in any way I can. I have just written this book so you have some answers, know what questions to ask and seek out the best and healthiest life saving methods out there.

THANK YOU for the following information:
This site has an extensive wealth of information and free downloads ..
EUROPEAN SOCIETY FOR MEDICAL ONCOLOGY
ESMO.ORG
Go to the link , they offer a FREE 32 page PDF patients guide on understanding IMMUNOTHERAPY SIDE EFFECTS.. this is practically a gift so if you're unsure there you go

http://www.esmo.org/Patients/Patient-Guides/Patient-Guide-on-Immunotherapy-Side-Effects

In this guide, you can find information about:

- The immune system and cancer
- The concept of immuno-oncology
- How does modern immunotherapy differ from chemotherapy and tumour-targeted drugs?
- What are the side effects of immunotherapy?
  ○ What symptoms should I look out for?
  ○ When are these side effects most likely to appear and how common are they?
- How will immunotherapy-related side effects be managed?
  ○ Management of most common immune-related side effects
  ○ Management of rare side effects

As well as :

THANK YOU for the following information:

RENO INTEGRATIVE MEDICAL CENTER
6110 Plumas St. Suite B
RENO NEVADA 89519
1-775-829-1009
WWW.RENOINTEGRATIVEMEDICALCENTER.COM

DCA = DICHLOROACETATE - safe chemical compound recently found to be useful in helping eliminate all kinds of cancer

SALICINIUM : natural based plant extract, complex sugar molecule, harmless to normal cells, will only affect ANAROBIC cells destroying the enzymatic cloak which ALLOWS to hide from the immune system.

IPT- INSULIN POTENTIAL THERAPY:
It's job is to drop level of BLOOD SUGAR once level is dropped opens up their cell membranes to catch any SUGAR MOLECULES through the blood hence it's a *SMARTBOMB*

DENDRITIC CELL VACCINE:
Removes t'cells- reintroduces back into the body AGGRESSIVE CANCER KILLER will help and aid, communicates with other T'CELLS to MULTIPLY pass info to the other T'CELLS much like *WNT-SIGNALING* explained earlier AUTO-CRINE-PARA-CRINE

U.B.I. THERAPY: ULTRA VIOLET IRRIDATION able to do 6 things
    1. kills bacteria/viruses
    2. Super charges immune system
    3. Improves circulation
    4. Oxygenation of tissues
    5. Aids bodies tolerance towards radiation and chemo
    6. cardio vascular protection through increased power, anti –infection properties
CHELATION THERAPY:
Detoxifant used for removal of HEAVY METALS from the body thereby improving metabolic function, blood flow through blocked arteries

AQUA CHI THREATMENT:

Enhances the body's ability to DETOXIFY and HEAL, rebalances' amplifies bodies BIO- ELECTRIC FIELD enabling body to heal itself.

ELECTRIC FOODS wasn't this discussed in a previous chapter, your body does not run on SUGAR it runs on ELECTRICITY....HELLO

HYPERTHERMIA THERAPY:

Cancer HATES high heat, this one way of getting heat deep into tissues without undue comfort

Can use a FIRDOME PORTABLE

Interestingly enough through further research at the time I added this last edition while reading I came across two articles on SALICINIUM through THEFREELIBRARY.COM

A NEW NONTOXIC CANCER CO-TREATMENT

and

SALICINIUM: induced apoptosis and phagocytosis of circulating tumor cells and cancer stem cells

Apoptosis is a naturally occurring process in the body. Cells that become damaged may need to commit suicide in order to avoid causing harm to other cells.

Phagocytosis - Time to Eat! Simply put, cells need to eat and drink just like you. Phagocytosis is the process of a cell eating

Both of these articles were written by: ROBERT A. ESLINGER
DO, HMD
BOARD OF HOMEOPATHIC MEDICAL EXAMINERS STATE
OF NEVADA
Author of:
OUTMANEUVER CANCER: A integrative doctors journey
Owner and Medical Director of Reno Integrative Medical
Center (RIMC) in Reno, NV.

Please visit the website of his medical center there's a wealth of information there.

RGCC TESTING
Research Genetic Cancer Center
WWW.RGCC.GENIELAB.COM
Greece Cancer Center Genetic research laboratory that has developed a PATENTED MEMBRANE that is able to capture MALIGNANT CELLS from your own blood.
1-678-947-4454
THE GENESISCENTER.COM

NOW FOR MY ACKNOWLEDGEMENTS TO DOCTORS I'VE READ ON PAPERS, CANCER CENTERS, I AM FOREVER GRATEFUL TO CONNECT WITH ALL OF YOU THROUGH MY OWN RESEARCH ON THE INTERNET THROUGH YOUR LECTURES, OR JUST COMING ACROSS YOUR NAME IN A NEWS ARTICLE, INTERVIEWS, ARTICLES IN MAGAZINES, IMMUNOLOGY REPORTS ETC, HERE ARE MY

WWW.RGCC.GROUP.COM
This lab offers PERSONALISED CANCER TESTING.
This used to be considered ONCOSTAT test also known as CHEMOSENSITIVITY TEST
The GREECE TEST will give you a much better indication of whether or not the chemo drugs will have any effect
You can see which natural therapies might be effective against your type of cancer.
There's also a genetic test involved to help identify which THERAPIES, CONVENTIONAL or ALTERNATIVE with
NEUTRACEUTICAL COMPOUNDS
May be affective against your type of cancer.
The beauty of all this is that you can find out before physically beginning treatment.
Test results are received within 10 business days.
Unfortunately this is not covered by insurance; a majority of Oncologist do not use the GREECE TEST. However this is a worthwhile investment.

NUTRACEUTICALS COMPOUNDS:

is any non toxic food component that has scientifically proven health benefits including TREATMENT OR PREVENTION.

You can download a free PDF-slide presentation under the same title online.

THANK YOUS

My first one is to DR. JOHN JAMES BRADSTREET may your memory live on, you gave me part of an answer
to a nearly impossible question!
DR. RUSSEL BLAYLOCK thank you. He lead and intrigued me with the CYTAKIND STORM – Dr. Blaylock has a number of books on health and wellness you can purchase on line, numerous articles he's written, I came across him while perusing VACCINE.ORG as well as www.blaylockreport.com

DR. DAVID NOAKES, CEO and FOUNDER of FIRST IMMUNO BIOTECH - you can look him up lead me to find the

EUROPEANLABORATORY.NL
EUROPEAN LABORATORY OF NUTRIENTS
In THE NETHERLANDS
Email: HYPERLINK "mailto:eln@healthdiagnostics.nl" eln@healthdiagnostics.nl

This laboratory as well as VITAMIN DIAGNOSTICS offers certain blood measurements for early detection.

also know as:

HEALTH DIAGNOSTICS AND RESEARCH INSTITUTE
H. D. R. I.
540 Bordentown Ave. Suite 2300
SOUTH AMBOY, NJ 08879
1-732-721-1234
Remember they only do request by PHYSICIANS and MEDICAL NUTRITIONIST, but now you have the resource info

These doctors were actually put in a bad light, I did decide to read up on all the negative rhetoric and why they were spoken about in that fashion however what they were being talked about wasn't really what I was interested in, that was just leading me to the bridge that connected me to some of the answers that I was looking for.

You can do your own research and read up on all their literature if you are interested in this information.

CENTER4CANCER.COM has a great article by Bill Sandi and Timothy Hubell speaking on DR. YAMAMOTO'S research titled VITAMIN D BINDING PROTEIN excellent article and if interested you can read and entire book that is extensive on Dr. Yamamoto's research on the following site: www.gcmaf.timsmithmd.com
HUGE THANK YOUS TO MY OTHER REFERENCES written within this book!
SCIENCEBLOG.CANCERRESEARCHUK.ORG
AMERICAN JOURNAL OF IMMUNOLOGY
JOURNAL OF ANTI-CANCER RESEARCH
ANOASISOFHEALING.COM
BREASTCANCERWELLNESS.ORG – blogged about
SALICINIUM homeopathic cancer treatment method that tricks cancer cells and destroys the cloak.
UNITEDPATIENTSGROUP.COM
LYRANARA.ME – article on GOLEIC- VITAMIN D by CHRISTINE SIEPE
WWW.CARNIVORA.COM

Dr. C. Joe Schneller M.D., N.D., D.Sc., D.Ac. D.C. Inventor of World's First Hybrid Darkfield Microscope performs preliminary study preceding double blind clinical study demonstrating how three Capsules of Carnivora wake up important white blood cells & NK cells of the immune system creating "Powerful Immune Defense

CARNIVORA: responds to abnormal cells only

http://carnivorahellas.com

you can read a full descriptive explanation on this site.

boosting your WHITE BLOOD CELLS helps in making them NATURAL KILLER CELLS, you need to understand an study the importance of WHITE BLOOD CELLS.

You can view: TEACHING YOUR IMMUNE SYSTEM TO RECOGNIZE CANCER and ELIMINATE IT on You Tube and also read the book 9 STEPS TO KEEP THE DOCTOR AWAY
Both by DR. RASHID BUTTAR

www.scotthealthsystem.com

VITAL BOOST ENERGY can be purchased on this site for $39.99

What does this do VitalBoost Energy Greens, is a natural good-tasting high-ORAC greens mix that assists the digestive system, supports immune-boosting functions, and provides the nutrients you need to boost natural energy. Our flagship product can be used on a daily basis long-term to promote the transition to a balanced healthy state for the body.

www.burtongoldberg.com

ALTERNATIVE MEDICINE/THE DEFINITIVE GUIDE

Cancer Conquest (DVD)

can be purchased at link above

www.ayuverdicscience.com

nutritional supplements that integrate and ayuverdic physicians use look up:

VIRENDER SOHDI ND, MD, AYURVED

Benefits of integrative cancer care: treatments and case studies

THE ALPHA LIPOIC ACID BREAKTHROUGH
By: BURT BERKSON
You can also get a free (pdf) article ALHA LIPOIC ACID-defending your liver! By Margi Squires

https://www.cancertutor.com/hydrazine/
HYDRAZINE SULFATE: eliminates extreme weight loss in cancer patients CACHEXIA stops LATIC ACID from turbo charging cancer

http://www.diversehealthservices.com/dhs-protocols/immune-health.html

R.E. Tent, D.C., N.D., Ph.D
Jeff Senechal, D.C., CFMP

This is a great resource site, he has great lengthy lectures that are informative some are a bit rough around the edges however; you need to take the good with the bad. I'm mostly interested in the care and well being of the mind and body this is what I'm truly looking for.

BRAVO-PROBIOTICS.COM

Can purchase a probiotic yogurt kit on this site and please read the full descriptive explanation
It is imperative to understand HEALTHY GUT and BRAIN CONNECTION
YOUTUBE: overcoming Candida, parasites and autism by Dr. Marco Ruggiero M.D. and CLIVE de CARLE interesting webinar a bit boring unless you're as inquisitive as I am, great explanations

If you take time to understand and educate yourself you will see the importance of taking care of your body during this time plays a big role. THE DECISIONS ARE YOURS TO MAKE

For example DR. NICHOLAS GONZALEZ had perfected a strict 3 part approach consisting in INDIVIDUALIZED DIETS in order to BALANCE their ACIDITY and ALKALINITY

1. KNOW YOUR BLOOD TYPE
2. INDIVIDUALIZED SUPPLEMENT REGIMEN
3. DETOXIFICATION REGIMENS

You need specific blood test that measure immune structure and function MAY HE REST.......AND THANK YOU for all your research it was not in vain!

PLEASE PAY CLOSE ATTENTION all this information is rather BASIC if you choose to do your own research and understand.............
You can have INCREDIBLE RESULTS to a normal life you just have to be committed!

In addition, if you do not believe me then you have not met MELISSA-PERSON ASHFORTH hers is a story of DETERMINATION, INSTINCT, HOPE and the maintaining the most important role of all FAITH IN GOD! She can be contacted below if interested in NUTRITIONAL FOODS, CLEAN EATING & HEALTHY LIVING while living with CANCER!
ARBONNE CONSULTANT ID:22086227
WWW.MELISSAPERSONASHFORTH.ARBONNE.COM
If interested subscribe to her channel on YOUTUBE MELISSA PERSON ASHFORTH CANCER JOURNEY 1 & 2

When I first started my journey writing this book, I kept coming across articles and interviews on people that were healing from cancer naturally. I read many stories on cancer survivors and remission but I kept praying to meet someone physically who healed completely.

Lo and Behold upon the first day of orientation at RUTGERS BUSINESS SCHOOL Melissa sat right next to me said hi and had the biggest smile on her face. When we had to introduce ourselves in front of the class she had revealed her story.

I could not believe it a STAGE 4 CANCER SURVIVOR was sitting right next to me. GOD sent me an ANGEL.

I LOVE SUGAR

I can't simplify this explanation enough, for you to understand. Again you can lead a horse to water but you cannot make them drink it!

One thing I truly despise is when there's a clip on the news like A CLOSER STEP TO THE CURE for CANCER and then they flash on the screen a picture of a CANCER CELL w/all these ARMS, all of a sudden they cut off and go into a LAB reporting on some promise that is not going to come through, for the average viewer you just lost them for someone like me I'm still stuck on that picture with that cancer cell with all those arms and this is how I'm looking at it WHAT IS THAT AND WHAT IS THE PURPOSE OF ALL THOSE ARMS? That's really the question I'm asking as you've read in this book there was a 'lot of talk about SUGAR and MAINTAINING a healthy IMMUNE SYSTEM... you see when that cancer cell once its formed,has done is create a city within itself to maintain its strength stays planted in that one place THOSE ARMS you see are arteries that have grown out to reach into the nearest BLOOD STREAM it's much like creating PLUMBING for a building or wiring for CABLE TV it has to go straight to the source and what the arms / arteries are doing once it's made its connection to the source is basically drawing and feeding itself THE SUGAR that is passing through the blood stream and this is how it maintains and intensifies it's strength. This is why you need to learn how TO STARVE IT, KILL IT without SUPPORTING IT with SUGAR. That means PASTA, BREAD, POTATOS, CAKES, PIES, and REFINED SUGAR ETC. This is their source just like a FIOS/CABLE wire needs to connect for you to watch TV so do these arteries on cancer cells NO DIFFERENT!

This can't be simplified enough this is why the average newspaper is at a 11th grade reading level there's a reason.

What I just explained is called ANGIOGENESIS
ANGIO- GENESIS consist of two words your clue is in these words just pay attention:

1. ANGIO definition is the latin greek word for STORAGE BOX, CONTAINER RECEPTICLE ETC.
2. GENESIS: you should all know what this means THE BIRTH, THE BEGINING

Reverse the meanings THE BIRTH/BEGINING OF A STORAGE BOX. Now ask the question WHAT IS IT STORING? I JUST TOLD YOU. SIMPLE MATH just need to pay attention

TO MY NIECES AND NEPHEWS

VANESSA, JEREMY, RICKY, JOSIE, EMILY, ZACHARY, LEILANI, JEREMIAH, NOAH, BRYSON and MATIAS

This is my legacy I leave to all of you and are to be responsible for, none of you have excuses between your GREAT GRANMA, GRANPA RICKY, UNCLE WENCE AND I you can see how truly gifted and talented we are each one of you carries a gift that extends from each of us until you are mature enough to be responsible of it, the talent won't come through I expect each and every one of you to go beyond what I have done you just read my story, with the exception of LILIA she's tending a garden full of pink and lavender roses the first ROSE lies in GRANDMAS living room with her secret note, she was going to be the botanist in our family.

A LITTLE EXTRA STORY TIME,
JUST FOR YOU BETSY

Think about it ,Health care costs to the roof that a majority can't even afford to pay

All this research, fundraising, search for a cure even with the medical advances and STILL NO CURE!

I've encountered enough women going through. Many explained how they felt with the meds, felt as if they had no hope, how Dr's were just making them feel like numbers and cattle, Scared or just going through the motions many and I mean many on fixed incomes, single, single mothers, sometimes no support system and others the husband blaming them for getting cancer, having affairs and only thinking with their penises I have sat through all of it!

I'll show you how the dot's are connected and how on earth did I become so inquisitive?

Many years ago one of my early jobs was working for the U.S. ATTORNEYS office and a Private Corporate Law Firm in NJ. I was fascinated with all the litigation and the law library. So much information to consume, when I was 1st hired at the corporate firm I was responsible for putting together their legal research library together, way before it was catalogued on your personal computer hundreds of books.

At the U.S. ATTORNEYS office I was a docket clerk, assistant to the paralegals, responsible to go into judge's chambers to drop off the cases before 4 p.m. and trust me it was timed I didn't get paid much however

I learned as much as I could at that age, but really my favorite part was delivering the mail to the F.B.I in the building, everyone got to know me and were friendly to me, I would end up talking to them and after a while I would notice they had boxes upon boxes of just picture posters, photos of people coming in and out of doors, windows, store fronts, corners things that made no sense to me at that time, I was around 19 or 20 , being inquisitive I just so happened to ask the question what was the purpose of those simple pictures and the majority was of investigative crimes trust me they were nothing to look at. But the one thing that stood out to me and has stuck with me till this day is *TRACE EVIDENCE* so one of them answered my question and said OZZY don't pay attention to the picture, pay attention to what's going on around the picture, pick up the little pieces around them . THIS STUCK.

So if I ever was to go into law it would have to be FORENSIC SCIENCE I love picking all the details apart and then bringing them all together, this is why WIG MAKING comes natural to me because of all the pieces.

So why all of this BABBLING?

I truly am a education junky, I tend to always occupy my idle time reading a lot of insightful books, listening to many boring lectures and watching as many uninteresting interviews along the way . What I'm usually doing is picking apart what is being said and observing body language when they are speaking.

We all have to start somewhere, WNT SIGNALING and understanding this triggered my research, I just needed to know how to piece it together without it sounding kooky.

The books I'm about to reference have absolutely no relation to one another however you'll see how well they are connected just like a bunch of disorganized cells!

We'll start with:

THE IMMORTAL LIFE OF HENRIETTA LACKS
By: REBECCA SKLOOT

An excellent book that includes interesting historical account on this woman's life. But I was looking for something specific within the book and WA'LA there it was TIMELINE, RAPID CELL DIVISION and the RELATIONSHIP between the AMERICAN and RUSSIAN DR'S that right there was it out of the entire book.

Well how special was this relationship? Well after reading this next book prior to THE IMMORTAL LIFE I had read

OPERATION PAPERCLIP
By: ANNE JACOBSON

Another excellent book in this book she explains the relationship between the American / Russian Dr's and scientist!

Many don't realize that upon the German/Nazi war being over AMERICA and RUSSIA were racing to see who will get to these DR'S and SCIENTIST 1st.

Many of these DR'S and SCIENTIST became heads of chemical and pharmaceutical companies throughout the world and a number of them right here in the U.S.

2 different books 2 different topics but totally well connected. I would love to be in the same room with these authors one day.

There are many other books that I have read to prove my theory, however I just wanted to KEEP IT SIMPLE

Was that enough STORY TIME for you BETSY?

THERES GOING TO BE MORE WHEN THIS KICKS IN K!

DEFINITIONS

ENZYME: are biological molecules (proteins) that act as catalysts and help complex reactions occur everywhere in life

LYSOSOMES: hold enzymes that were created by the cell.
The purpose of the lysosome is to digest things.

ALPHANACETYLGALACTOSAMINE: is an amino sugar derivative of galactose and necesseray for intercellular communication much like WNT SIGNALING.

GLYCOPROTEINS: provide many functions: they give structural support to cells help to form connective tissues

GLYCOLIPIDS: Their role is to maintain stability of the membrane and to facilitate cellular recognition

GALACTOSE: is a simple sugar, which belongs to simple carbohydrates. Galactose is composed of the same elements as glucose

CA MARKERS: CA125 test measures the amount of the protein (CANCER ANTIGEN 125) is in your blood.
A ca125 test may be used to monitor certain cancer during treatment, in some cases a ca125 test may be used to look up early signs of ovarian cancer in women with very high risk of the disease

ca125test-mayoclinic.org

IMMUNE STATUS: the ability of the body to demonstrate an immune response to defend itself against disease upon foreign substances
*medical dictionary / THEFREEDICTIONARY.COM

FOR BOOKINGS AND CLASSES
CONTACT
OZZY
WWW.OZZYSHAIRART.INFO
INFO@OZZYSHAIRART.INFO

LECTURE: HOW TO UNDERSTAND AND CATER TO A CLIENT WHO IS LOSING HER HAIR WHILE LIVING WITH CANCER!

CLASSES

How to get involved in the hair replacement and trichology field, in this class you will learn:

1. How to understand human hair wig making and design
2. How to make minor repairs
3. How to alter wigs to suit the client's needs
4. Proper methods of attachments
5. How to outsource synthetic wig companies and open accounts
6. Which are my top trusted international manufactures.
7. How to outsource hair
8. How to communicate effectively in the International Hair business.
9. Who are my go to middle men / companies in the U.S. if you don't understand international wig making.
10. How to outsource wholesale attachment methods, medical glue, tapes etc.

THE HAIR REPLACEMENT COURSE CONSISTS OF A 3 DAY CLASS, I WILL BE FRANK WITH YOU IT IS AN INTENSE CLASS, IT WILL BE A LOT OF INFORMATION TO ABSORB AND IT NEEDS TO BE TAUGHT IN A MANNER THAT WILL BE EASY TO UNDERSTAND.

THIS IS NOT FOR SOMEONE WHO IS OUT TO GET A QUICK BUCK AND THINK THEY ARE GOING TO GET RICH OVERNIGHT.

THE HAIR REPLACEMENT COURSE IS ONLY TAUGHT

IN SMALL GROUPS SO YOU WILL BE ABLE TO GET MY UNDIVIDED ATTENTION NO MORE THAN 10 PEOPLE.

Also included will be all my go to sources that help in filling out all the gaps.

There's a 'lot you can learn and benefit from if you are dedicated and like to work hard.

YOU CAN FOLLOW ME ON:

OZZYS HAIR ART on FACEBOOK

HAIRLOSSSOLUTIONSBYOZ on INSTAGRAM

OZZY@OZZYSHAIRART on TWITTER

OZZY VERA on LINKED IN

FINALLY DONE, 1 WEEK AFTER HURRICANE MARIA WENT THROUGH PUERTO RICO MY BEAUTIFUL ISLAND THAT WILL NEVER BE THE SAME.

PUERTO RICAN AND PROUD!

WE CAN ONLY MOVE FORWARD

THE LORD GIVETH AND THE LORD TAKETH AWAY …..BLESSED BE THE NAME OF THE LORD ALL DAY LONG……….

In closing this book is for educational purposes certain chapters within this book are not intended to stir or cause debate, matter of fact all this Is PUBLIC INFORMATION, the books that I have referenced are not meant to stir fear into you actually whatever seems negative it actually ended having a POSITIVE OUTCOME without the negative we wouldn't have many of the BRILLIANT Dr's, Chemist or Scientist that exist.

My intentions are to really ease the psychological burden when making a decision on HER NEW HAIR.

I truly believe we all hold a key to the door that holds the ANSWER.

My goal is to fill a very HUGE GAP that lives within leaving the clinic where the patient is being treated to when they need to purchase hair.

THIS IS MY DEBATE and ARGUMENT!.

This is why my book was written this is my TRIBUTE to MY AUNT and this is where my ARGUMENT will REMAIN!

Printed in the United States
By Bookmasters